Retire Well!

I0471625

DJ Charpentier

BRUSHNECK COVE PRESS

Warwick, Rhode Island

Cover photo by: Pat Charpentier

For Pat, still riding together

Other Books by DJ Charpentier

Fiction
Reggie Slater Mystery Series
Bethany Blues
Ocean City Blues
Key West Blues

Russ Deever Mystery Series
Beach Blues
Carousel Blues
Marginal Blues

Nonfiction
As Luck Would Have It...Changing Your Mind:
A Practical Guide to Retirement
First Edition & Second Edition
As Luck Would Have It...5-Years Later
Retire Well!

All titles are available for Kindle or in print at
Amazon.com

This is a work of non-fiction. My wife Pat and I started our retirement at 60 years old. We are now in our ninth year of freedom and adventure. Our story is shared here to give you the confidence that you can do it, too.

Table of Contents

Preface

It has been over nine years since my wife, Pat, and I both retired at age 60; which some might think of as *early* retirement. Looking back and considering our experiences for this, the third time, I think there are some different perspectives from this point in time, both financial and emotional, than I first thought or anticipated in the first or second writing of this manuscript. You know what they say about making plans...*and then life happens and God laughs*. That is what invokes fear in the hearts and minds of those contemplating the leap into retirement; the uncertainty. What everyone asks and retirees talk about is: *"How is it going?" Is the money holding out? How are you and your wife getting along? How did that period of adjustment go? Are you doing some different things with your money and the big thing...what do you do all day? What adjustments are you going to make?* There is the constant questioning; even in your own mind about...did I do the right thing?

We retirees are a cooperative and chatty lot. It's not like when you were working and your paycheck and financial matters seemed to be highly protected state secrets. I don't know why, but it just seemed that way. Now, everyone knows that only a fool doesn't share information. The retiree's social network is paramount. We don't have HR anymore to manage our affairs or take care of our benefits. All we have is each other. We talk about the pitfalls we have encountered and how we maneuver around a system that seemingly plots against us; first with, "press 1 for English," and then "Your call is important to us." We are constantly bombarded with different health programs and annuity schemes on TV making us question our situation. Every year Medicare prompts us to review our benefits and make sure we are covered. The programs change, the coverage changes, and it is *open season*. What is a person to do?

But I shouldn't and I won't complain. All it takes to navigate this quagmire of things that must be done in retirement is patience and fortitude; two things of which we have plenty of...it is best not to fool with an informed senior citizen as many companies have found. We are determined, vocal, have plenty of time, and a grand network.

The first edition of this book was completed as we finished our third year of retirement; the second at five years, and now it is moving toward ten years since we launched this adventure; our second phase. The initial writing outlined how we got to retirement at age 60. Next, it was hitting that all important age, 65. Things were going well and it seemed that we were set. No, no, no... when you hit 65 the world changes; especially with health care. Medicare intervenes and depending on what you are carrying into retirement from your employment or coverage you personally have, Medicare makes it different. And now nine years into it; there are other issues with family, relatives, and friends that prompt the writing of this continuing saga in an ever changing environment.

Also, I'm now looking back from even later in retirement to evaluate what I (we) did financially. It seems we were solid, but we have already replaced our aging motor home and now I'm thinking about the cars. These are big expenses that were formerly financed by paychecks and loans over time, but now have to be financed using withdrawals from our monthly retirement checks and/or our nest egg. Now what? And now there are new desires for our family's future...the purchase of a lake house of all things; much more on that later.

We're getting older and surely not as quick witted as we once were. Should I consider getting a financial advisor now? I was organized and keeping up with my stuff, but now it seems I have too much to do! What with traveling and all...I just don't always keep up. They say when you get older, your sharpness in dealing with these matters declines. One thing I do know is that it sure takes longer to do things. I still have not established the trust I intended to get to...I really need to do that. So, I'll talk about the financial advisor that I have hired and the advantages and disadvantages of that move.

I'm a few years down the road from retirement and my personal connections sure have changed. I'm seeing more people than ever. That requires some regulation or it will destroy (is destroying) my waistline. It has been great fun seeking out old friends and I never pass up an opportunity to get together with them; if I can help it.

So, we retired at 60 and we're having a great time. We spend much of the year at home and at the nearby lake house, but we travel extensively in our motor home. How is all this working out after nine years? I postulated that we had encountered the "Ball of Confusion" in heading into retirement. Had we done it right? Were all the bases covered? What did I miss? These were all questions I pondered in the *"As Luck Would Have It."* I thought I had answered those questions in ...*5 Years Later*, but there is a changing landscape or an awaiting tsunami somewhere down the road that might change everything. We have bit into the golden egg of retirement and seemingly, I don't yet have yoke all over my face, but I'm still digging some shell fragments out of the mix.

Chapter 1: Forgetting What You Know
And becoming something else...

Do you know who you are? The day after you retire, you're going to be someone or at least something else. Just think...You're at a party and someone asks you, "What do you do?" Today, working at your job, you know that answer. I'm a lawyer, accountant, teacher, mechanic, college professor, bricklayer, carpenter, etc. But the day after you retire you answer, "Err." Think about it. Who/what are you? Are you defined by your job so much so that you are not anything else? What will be your emotional identity after you retire? This is a question that is more essential to your happiness in retirement than the retirement annuity or nest egg you have saved in your working years. This question deserves at least as much consideration, if not more, than your financial plan. So, let's consider the answer to that question first, before we get to the money part.

Throughout our lives we are identified by what we do. But is that what you/we really are? It never really has been but most of us, at least I didn't, give it a lot of thought outside of answering, "I'm a school principal." That works great until the day you retire and the next day, you're not. So, now what are you? Strip away what you do and what are you?

You are "retired" is the new answer, but what does that mean? You are now a father, mother, husband, wife, grandfather, grandmother, brother, sister; son, daughter, painter, art lover, writer, musician, traveler, fisherman, and you maybe do volunteer work or work part-time really many of the things you have been all along. The possibilities are endless. It's a whole new world and a whole new life. And after you have been in it for awhile, you realize that no one cares what you did in your former life, just who you are now at this moment as you stand in front of them. Are you friendly? Are you a person they want to talk to? All of a sudden you are not placed in a pigeon hole of what you do and all of the expectations that go with that. You are just a person...an equal...and you go from there. It's really a bit scary at first and then enlightening, if you ask me.

You are completely reinvented in retirement and it may be the biggest, most free-choice situation of your life outside of your career... Your money (we'll get to that later) now is a vehicle to do what you want to do...maybe what you always really wanted to do; not what you are told or instructed to do. The pressures of career and family are in your past. As they say, you are now the master of your universe. What do you want it to look like? (Sorry, can't do anything about that thinning hair.) What do you want to be now that you're grown up? This is best thought about well before you retire. You do not want to get out of bed that first morning of your new life in retirement, look in the mirror and say, "Now what?"

Nowhere was this more apparent for me then after I was made a school administrator. I had become one of 42 administrators in the school district instead of one of over 1100+ teachers. There were people that would hardly give me the time of day before that moment. There were places that were off limits...oh, not formally, but everybody knew that you did not belong there. Suddenly, all of that was gone. I didn't feel any different. I didn't act any different. People just treated me differently because of who I now was. I don't think I ever and still don't fully understand it, but all of a sudden I was redefined. And worse I was not defined by what I truly was, but what I did and I was that...right up to the last day I worked and then the day after I retired...I wasn't.

So, this is something you have to consider when you retire or best well before that. What am I? What do I really want to do? It is best to start early because if you are defined by what you do and then you no longer do it, what are you? I can see this leading to a feeling of depression after a time and I'm not sure some people ever figure it out as they sit in their recliners watching TV mindlessly as the years tick away. Now, I know you don't want that kind of an existence, but if you cannot figure out what you want to do, it may become your default.

The message here is to think about what you want to do in your retirement before you are retired. Make up the new definition of what you want to be. Then, when you are no longer defined by what you "do," you now are what the future *you* will be even before you retire. That new mindset is unbelievably liberating. The point is that when you retire you are not quitting what you are presently doing; but rather deciding to do something else with your life. Deciding that this thing that defines you now, no longer does, and I'm going to stop being that person and do this now. If you can't do that, than I feel that retirement is a quitting...and where do you go from there?

You are not alone on this journey and there are several books and web sites to help you along with the thought process. There are magazines like "AARP" monthly and such that discuss these issues all the time. AARP sponsors a website called "Life Reimagined" that is very helpful in structuring your retirement. Real people talk about their experiences and share their successes and failures in this process. Seek out these sites and magazines and "take note." This may be the most important self-help course you have ever been involved in. After all, your happiness in retirement is at stake. In researching material for this rewrite, I have found that "Life Re-imagined" sometimes know as "My Next Phase" has since become a movement with many contributors all jumping on the bandwagon of retiring baby boomers and charging for their advice.

When we decided to retire, we knew we were at the end of our profession. How do you know? You can feel it in your bones. We had talked about what we wanted to do; we even tried it out (more on this later). The decision after a time became obvious, the money and the health care were in place (more on this later, too) and it was time to go. So we forgot what we were and concentrated on what we were going to be and set forth on a different adventure, together. And we have never looked back. Almost ten years later, we still do not regret our decision...not for a second.

Chapter 2: Is There More?

To infinity…and beyond…!

You bet there is! There is everything after retirement that you have dreamed about in your life and more. But when you're told you can do anything you want, it feels great, but where do you start? What do you do first? You can become "frozen in freedom" and not know what to do and thereby do nothing at all. So, at least two years before you make that decision concerning your final date of retirement, you need to do some serious thinking, research, and have a few heart-to-heart talks with your spouse. Oh, yes. This is not your decision alone. That partner you have is facing the same dilemma as you are and you both need help and cooperation to get it right.

Just like making financial decisions, you are not alone in this wrangling about what to do with the rest of your life. There are plenty of other souls out there, including your spouse, wringing their hands over the same type of decisions you are. Seek them out and talk to them. Ask them questions. First, start with those in your work place. What are they thinking? What plans have they made? You may find that some of them are reluctant to talk about personal financial matters, but they will open up about their future retirement plans, maybe not with specific dates and such, but with what they are going to do. Those that trust you more will talk about finances, as well. Don't forget about talking to your HR department to find out exactly how your retirement plan works and what you can expect in the way of support, if any, from the company.

Ask your colleagues what they are doing and thinking. Are they considering selling their house and moving to a new, maybe more tax friendly, location? What is their logic? Do they have a pension or just a nest egg? Taxes, especially income taxes, really do matter. If you are staying in the country, federal taxes can be minimized at best, but state income and sales taxes can be altogether eliminated by moving. I talked to one retiree that has a retirement home in another state for free. Why does he call it free and how can that be? Well, we live in a state that taxes pensions as ordinary income along with local taxes for your vehicles. He moved to another state that does not tax pensions as income and he declared residency there.

Declaring residency means he lives at least 6 months in the tax friendly state and files his taxes there...he can also live in his original state for six months where his family is. Of course he comes north for the summer and south for the winter. The money he saves in state and local taxes by declaring the tax friendly state as his state of residence pays for his second home. He not only saves on income taxes, but vehicle taxes as well...just by changing his state of residence. Looking at my recent tax bills, this is about $6,000 per year or $60,000 over 10 years. Many modular homes can be had for this amount or less in the southern states. So, my friend feels that his home in the tax friendly state is free.

Frequently, recent retirees of the same profession meet for coffee once a month for camaraderie and to reminisce. Maybe it would be worthwhile to seek out a group such as this that of course you are not yet a part of. Conversation with former work buddies can fill a void left by walking away from what you have done for years. It also gives you a circle of friends because many friends that you do have are still involved in work and don't yet have the freedom that you do. I find talking to these people a great comfort. They are also a great source of information. They have already taken the leap and know what pitfalls may await. They know the procedures and may help to walk you through them. These folks have already tried it out for awhile and may have some very worthwhile advice.

What about all that time you used to spend at work, what are you going to do with it now? Sure, you could say that now you are going to relax and decompress. You certainly deserve it after all of those years of getting up early, working late, and keeping your nose to the grindstone. But keeping your feet up on the ottoman and watching TV gets old after awhile; not to mention clogging your arteries and rotting your brain cells. And remember, you are not alone in this. Your spouse may have some other ideas that you need to listen to. Well, at least you better listen, because you will be spending a lot more time in each other's presence during retirement. There will be more on that later, too.

So, how will you figure out what to do with your time? There are several ways to do this but for me, just like when I was working, I made a plan. Yes, using the same skills that you already have and used during your work life is not an evil thing. Future planning and long term projects were my forte during my work life so; I used those skills to plan my retirement life as well. Not to say that I knew it all and made a plan cast in stone...but it certainly gave me/us a place to start. Certainly you can make a list of maintenance and repairs needed to your own property and make a schedule to accomplish that.

Branching out further, I searched the internet for "retirement plans" as a place to start. I came up with a site called "My Next Phase." I had also seen this in one of the magazines I receive. The site was a great help. There were many profile questions and from the answers, possible retirement "activities," including work were suggested. It was sort of an aptitude test, but it measured not only ability but what you like to do...because that is what retirement is...doing what you like, not what you have to do. You can take some of your skills or learn new skills and turn them into second careers as many have done. The point is you do work that you want and enjoy...that's not labor, but joyful work. If you make some money at your new found profession, great, but it is not necessary, because you have already planned for your income in retirement. You could work for free because it is something you believe in and want to do.

What did I want to do? And what did I need to do? Yes, I live in a house and maintain it (More on this later, too.) so I needed to plan time for maintenance tasks. First, about the house; I really have two of them: a residence with a street address and a motor home and they both need upkeep. Since the first writing, I also have a lake house that requires looking after. The motor home needs washing, waxing, minor maintenance (which I do myself), tires, and major maintenance which I have done by a local garage. I also had to take into consideration that I was going to use the motor home more in retirement so I would have to up the frequency of maintenance needs and plan for the expense. In keeping with my make-up, I made a list. Things I could do and things I had to have done...and how much that costs. Also, I wrote all of that down in a maintenance log that I keep for my motor home.

Then, there is my residence and the lake house. Yes, now that the kids are grown, out of the house, and on their own; the house it is a bit larger than we need. But, it has a nice view of the water and we love living there. It is also near the grandchildren. So, with those considerations, as a mutual decision, we're staying put. This was learned in one of those heart-to-hearts with my wife. I pretty much agreed, but the property needs some work that we had neglected in the later part of my work career.

So, again, I (we) made a list of needed repairs and things we wanted to do to the property to make it work for our retirement life. First, we needed interior repairs, carpets, paint, etc. Also, there are the former children's rooms that are now grandchild sleepover rooms. Those rooms also needed a change in furniture to accommodate their new function. We set about listing and prioritizing all of that. The grandchildren are growing up fast and no longer sleepover as much as they used to. That caused other changes as my wife moved some of her sewing/crafting activities from a basement room to one of the spare bedrooms; nothing is permanent.

Then, there was the outside. We had a falling down shed, a roof that was questionable, and some landscaping that we had wanted to do for years. We listed and prioritized all of that. Let me say right here before I get into hot water, that I was not alone in this. The planning and the doing are a joint venture with my wife. She is always willing to help and she is an outside girl by nature so the gardens and much of the landscaping fell to her. She also pitches in on the painting tasks and I must say that she wears it well.

All right all you equal rights types...stop tisk, tisk, tisking me. She wants to do those things. In every relationship there is a division of labor that works. That division is not all the same for every couple and I couldn't make a list that works for us all of the time much less for any other couple. There are things we each like to do that don't fall into traditional roles and there are some that do...there are also things that neither of us likes to do, but we bite the bullet at times and just do it. It works for us...no apology necessary.

The inside and outside work was a daunting list. Add to that, things always come up that need doing right now that upset the best of plans. We looked at the list as a long-time project. And then you could add to that some more, we planned to take a couple of long-term trips in the motor home every year and continue weekend camping with our camping club. So, we refined the list some more and divided it into annual segments...also seasonal to meet inside and outside weather requirements.

And so we began. The lists have been revised many times, but we continue to plug away. I must say that the place is looking pretty good. I'm just waiting for what might break next. Also, new ideas have arisen and been added to the list; some by me and some by my wife. This has allowed me to verify the information imparted by my Dad for the first edition of this book.

I asked my Dad, who had maintained his home as I do and worked in his yard every day until he no longer could, if the list ever ends. The short answer he gave me was, "No." I said to him, "I thought there would be a moment when I would get caught up." Again, he said, "No, when you die, someone just takes over the list." I guess I'll keep going for as long as I can and someday; someone else can take over my list as we have taken over Dad's since his passing.

And then we have come to the point where some of the projects are just too big for us to handle. Oh, we used to be able to do some of them, but there is this thing that happens as you age and you just can't handle them anymore. Also, you make up your mind to travel and you just don't have the time. So, in order to get some things done, we hired someone to do them. I had done so many things myself over the years that this is a bit foreign to me, but I like the travel so I gave in.

The lake house could be described as "neglected" when we purchased it. If we had about caught up on home maintenance, this started the process anew. The first year we tackled the inside. Then, once we were comfy, we had a new extension built on to our dock by a local worker, but we repainted the dock and deck at the waterfront. We rebuilt the shed and painted that. We had a new roof put on the house and are presently repainting the outside. Yes, we work a lot at the lake, but what we do improves the property and will make it last for our family.

And then, as I mentioned above, there is the travel.

Throughout my life and I'll bet yours, the words were uttered, "If I only had the time." Well now you do. From that hobby you always wanted to learn to those places you always wanted to visit. Now, you've got the time for it all! The only snafu to all of this is that it costs. We'll talk about that later when we discuss finances in your retirement but for now, let's assume you have the cash that you need.

When the Mrs. and I had the "big talk," motor home travel was one of the things we wanted to do. We didn't ever have a Chevrolet, but we still wanted to see the USA. I offered foreign trips to my wife, but she had little interest. I had tasted overseas travel while in the military and found it fascinating. I'll keep tempting her; maybe someday she will give in.

During our planning of retirement finances, part of the decision and planning was how much discretionary money every month we would have. That is beyond expenses, what can we spend on ourselves?

We found out during our "practice periods" (more on that later, too), that we can live cheaper on the road in our motor home than we can in our residence even if we continued to maintain that residence. So, our motor home travel is a no brainer. Because of electronic banking and bill pay, we can travel for any amount of time we want...two months...three months...or more and the world continues without us. And the funny thing that happens is just when you think you might blow through your discretionary funds for the month, lo and behold, on the first of the month, the checkbook gets filled back up and you can start again. There is a lot more on how to make this happen for you in another section.

Two or three times a year, we hit the road for a month or more. Where do we go? It's a big country and we're also attached to Canada, another big country. Trip planning again is a partnership. In partnership travel, it is essential that each of the partners is willing to tolerate some of the likes of the other even if it is not their favorite thing to do. If it is something one of you likes and the other doesn't, just find something else to do for awhile. It keeps the bruises down. For instance, I like to go to NASCAR races. My wife can take it or leave it, but she knows how to make the best of it when we go and its fun for the both of us. She likes to stop at quilt shops...I find something else to do. She crafts. I write. She can always plan a craft while I do that thing that I do and I usually carry my computer or something to read for waiting on the swing outside of the craft or quilt shop while she buys yet another project kit.

If you are traveling for a month, be sure to ascertain what is happening during that month with family and friends and that you are clear to go. If one of you is pining to be home and missing some family activity, the trip is going to be a rough one. You need to experience the freedom to feel the joy. Remember this is what you have been waiting for. The ties to family do not stop at retirement. If anything, it increases and you have to account for that deeper relationship in that time. If you do, you will enjoy your parents, children, and grandchildren much more.

If we decide to travel to a certain area, we both look at that area for things we would like to do or see. We do this separately at first and then start talking about it together. I'm usually the planner of the route and my wife is in charge of accommodations. That's generally how it goes, but I get involved in the where to stay occasionally and surely I count on her to monitor our location on the map as we move along. As far as what happens when we get there, we both throw out ideas as we look through brochures etc. and then make some decisions. Checking out local activities and campgrounds on a smart phone has made planning much easier.

As we travel, we are generally pretty loose. Some people need to have reservations for everywhere they are going and are very apprehensive if they don't. The planning as we go is part of the adventure for us. As we head for a far flung destination, about noon time I'll know about how far we are going to get. During lunch, we talk about where to stay for the night and my wife gets on the cell phone and generally gets us the reservation that we want. Then, we bed down for the night and discuss the next day. This keeps us from looking too far ahead and getting confused about new places and destinations. For some of the more popular tourist spots, we'll call several days ahead to insure we get a camping spot. If others are involved in our plans, we need to stick closer to a schedule.

These are some of the routine and not so routine things that work for us, but this is our retirement I'm talking about. I'm just trying to lay out a general plan so that you too can plan your retirement life because up to now much of your life...at least 10 or 12 hours per day has been planned for you. Now, you are the boss...this is your chance...your time...and your desire to be what you have always wanted.

I don't pretend to know what will satisfy you in retirement but I/we love the travel, but sometimes it is not enough. We both started thinking about filling some of our time by helping others. Neither of us could really decide what we wanted to do...what we did know is that we didn't want to do what we had done before. We had been there and done that and (I tried it once on a consulting basis) didn't want to do it again. We also didn't want to get tied down for long periods of time...the travel you know.

For me one opportunity came in a discussion with a fellow at church. He described to me his work with an organization called VITA. This volunteer group, official agents of the IRS, prepares tax returns for people making less than $55K per year. This happens during the tax season (winter)...perfect for me and my travel schedule! So, this is very satisfying for me and it helps many people out. There are sundry opportunities out there...you just have to look. I know other friends that volunteer time for food banks, thrift stores, and other charitable organizations. This also keeps your social network alive and growing.

My wife is and has always been a crafter. Her father worked with stained glass. After his passing, she inherited his stained glass tools and took a course to learn the craft. She now spends hours in her craft room making beautiful stained glass ornaments and flower garden pieces. This is in addition to her sewing and hand crafting activities...she keeps busy.

And then opportunity seeks you out. I have always been good with budgets. (Part of my old job) One opportunity arose with my church and I now serve on the board doing what else...budgets. This is a great mental exercise for me and I do enjoy it.

As I mentioned above, I once worked in a school for a short time as an administrator after I retired. I did this because it was a school that integrated the performing arts with standard academics and the opportunity intrigued me. At the end of my stint, Andy, one of the teachers looked at me and said, "You'll be back." Trinity Academy for the Performing Arts is a charter school in Providence, Rhode Island. I have since served as President of the Board of Trustees. I now mentor the Head of School and participate in the School Improvement Team. If you would like to support young artists, check out our website. It is the things that interest you that deserve your attention. They will also bring you great joy and satisfaction.

This all leads to the old adage, "How did I ever do this while I was working?" The answer is; you didn't. You did what you had to do to keep things going. Most home repairs/work was done on the weekends and you sliced out a bit of time for yourself. Now, you are going to slice out a big chunk of time for yourself and time to do the work you need to do around the house. By all that giving you did all of those years...not to say you did not enjoy it, but you were always striving for something else...well, now the something else is here so give yourself permission to enjoy it.

Consider yourself now *independently wealthy* because you are. If you planned it right, money comes to you every month and you don't have to work for it. Your time is yours to do with what you wish. Never thought you would be rich...well, how about that...now you are. If rich is having the money to support you in doing what you want to do, you are. Isn't it wonderful?

Chapter 3: What about Today?
Now what?

If you can do anything you want now that you are retired; sometimes that leads to what I'll call *freedom paralysis*. That is; there are so many choices, that it's too, too much and you never decide what to do. Later you say, "We should have done this? And now it's too late." This much freedom can make you giddy, you have to make some plans about your life. There are short-term plans including daily plans with your wife and without her. Then there are long-term plans like a trip to Florida for the winter and then there is the problem of what do I do...today. Let's talk about each of those, one at a time.

My wife and I retired in the same year, but not at the same time. She retired in June and I in mid-August. The reason for this is that she was a classroom teacher and her work year ended in June...also her birthday was in February so she was "of age" according to the rules at the end of the academic year. I was a school administrator so my work year was continuous and my birthday is in June so I retired in August. Just before I retired, my wife's Dad took sick and she had to travel to Arizona to be with him and her Mom. I was still working for a few more weeks, so I remained at home. Just as I retired, a hurricane struck our area. Our house and city were spared any significant damage, but the electrical power was out for four days; not that much of a hardship for me as you will see when you read further.

As I've mentioned, we have a motor home and it resides in our driveway when we are not traveling. This is a completely self-contained "Class A" unit equipped with a generator. With working appliances in the motor home and no electricity in the house because of the hurricane, I transferred much of the contents from our refrigerator in the house to the motor home and I moved in ...to the motor home that is. I found myself not having to work anymore with no electrical power in my house, and living alone in my motor home in my driveway and my wife was away. Talk about a change in lifestyle!

Yet, I had everything I needed. Food, water, electrical power, means to cook my food, and entertainment. So, for that week I developed a lifestyle that revolved around no one but me. I cooked my own food, watched TV when I wanted to (self-contained unit remember), went to visit my parents, and went to the car races. What a life! When the power came back on, I moved back into the house and continued my new found freedom ride...and then my wife came home.

A funny thing had happened while I was finishing up my working life. Since retiring in June, Pat had developed her own retirement lifestyle. And there we were...I with my freedom-bachelor-lifestyle and she was the bachelorette with a lifestyle all her own...and now we were living together, 24 hours per day, in the same house; surely a recipe for disaster.

This was a very awkward situation and the clash of the titans was on. It didn't take long to come to a head and we both realized what had happened. We had made plans, but life, as it often does, had intervened and now here we were in a new situation totally unprepared! We had a bit of a talk and started our retirement life together...we started over. We got in the camper and went away for a few days, something we knew how to do and talked it out.

One of the things we did after we returned home was establish a day out; together. Friday would be our day to do something as a couple. It had always been our date night so now it just became our "date day." We had used "date-night" to preserve our sanity and our marriage while the kids were growing up. Date night had become date morning (breakfast) during the hurried teenage years. By then our sanity was at stake along with our marriage. Any of you who have lived through the teenage years with your children know what I'm talking about.

Anyway, back to what to do today. I had read somewhere that a couple had faced a similar situation and had concocted a plan to put a map of the local area on the table and with their eyes closed; drop a coin on it. Wherever the coin landed, that's where they would go for the day. And so we tried it. The first time, the coin landed in the middle of a huge lake, a reservoir really. The town that was nearest to the lake was about 100 miles away from our home so we packed up the car and set out. It was a wonderful day. The reservoir was owned by the nearby state and around it was actually a park. There were walks and trails and tall towers to climb with wonderful views. We found the local diner and had a great lunch. We continued this ritual for a while and it helped us to adapt to our new life.

We fell into somewhat of a daily routine after we had established independent routines. I worked on projects around the house and hobbies. Pat did the same. Some things we did together and some things we did independently. This continues to be our daily routine even now. We each also have independent things we do with our friends outside the house.

My wife meets with her old work group once each month and I meet with a group of retired principals. We each have one-on-one friends that we treasure and I/we go to see my Mom every week as I did before my Dad passed...sometimes my wife comes along...at times she is busy with other things. As my Mom has aged we have increased our visits to twice per week.

It is not important what you both do every day, but it is important that; 1.) You do some things together, and 2.) You each have a somewhat independent life. This is not much different than when you were working except much of what you did then was defined by work and your work day. Now, you are the initiator so don't fall prey to the idleness of the couch and the ottoman. Get up and do something. Your life will be much more fulfilling and you will never be bored.

This has changed and expanded over the last nine years. I have some official duties in my positions, but continue my informal meetings with friends. My wife maintains her relationships with her work groups. We don't always take day trips on Fridays, but we do go out for lunch. This has changed somewhat because we travel much more than we used to. Constant adaptation...things change all the time.

New developments lead to additional things to do. As is evident by this third rewrite of As *Luck Would Have It,* I continue to write. I have now also written six novels: *Bethany Blues,* a story of a guy named Reggie that retires to Bethany Beach, Delaware, and gets tangled up in some intrigue with an ex-cop from Philadelphia; and *Beach Blues* a story of Russ and Sophia who live in Rhode Island. I have expanded each of these story lines into two more novels each. I have had great fun writing these books and wish I had started writing many years ago, but I don't know if my mind was quiet enough to be creative while I was working.

I also hooked up with a friend whose retirement dream was to produce music. He set up a digital recording studio in his house and invited me down to do some recording. This was a very humbling experience...hearing yourself playing guitar and singing...it truly does make you a better performer. We have finished an album and there are enough songs "in the can" to work on putting another one together. Time will tell.

Speaking of performing, I have also joined another old friend in performing live music. We call ourselves *JustUs* and perform locally for parties and gatherings. We have had great fun doing this and evidently we are pretty good because we keep getting work. Our only problem is that we are too tired to perform beyond eight in the evening so late night gigs are out. However, he is retiring soon so we'll see what changes that brings.

...And that is how you can fill up your day.

That's enough talk about the everyday...how about doing big things together? Things like trips and cruises, the eternal vacation? I would think that by the time you reach retirement age, you would both know something about each other's likes and dislikes about travel. Remember that big conversation? You did have it! This is where all that talking pays off. Taking what you know about each other and what you learned in the big talk, plan something you have really wanted to do as your first big vacation...well, you really can't call it a vacation anymore, you don't work remember, it is your life now so, let's call it your first big retirement adventure.

The fall after we retired I read about a celebration called the *Festival of Lights* in Gatlinburg, Tennessee. I showed to my wife and we just decided, "Why not?" So, we loaded up the camper and took off. The *Festival of Lights* is a Christmas display of over a million lights in Gatlinburg. If any of you know the area, Gatlinburg is adjacent to the *Great Smokey Mountain National Park*. It is also home to *Dollywood* and a great many country music shows. We took part in all of them and had a great time for a week.

And again...you don't work anymore. So, you would think that life is one big vacation. But let's get back to reality. There are still responsibilities: house, car, lawn, and doctor's visits...things that must be done plus events you both really want to do. Don't forget to schedule these appointments and responsibilities so that they don't interfere with long periods of freedom. If you have doctor's appointments popping up every week, how are you going to schedule those big adventures? It is best to plan those adventure periods of time and fit those other "must do" things in between. Remember, you are in control of your time. Don't let something like appointments control you. That's how it was when you worked. And you surely don't want to go back to that!

The only limiting factors to your adventures are time and money. You have already figured how much you can afford because you know your discretionary spending amount...the plan, remember. And there are limiting factors on your time...there is family...other commitments...that wedding you have to attend (You can turn that into a fun trip, too.). Anyway, figure out where and when and then plan to have a great time...and while you're on this adventure, talk about the next one. There is something really great about having a big thing to look forward to in your life...come to think of it, that's true whether you are retired or not.

A word of caution, don't fall into the trap of buying that vacation home or condo right away. While it may sound idyllic, you need to try it first. That beach community you have visited several times on vacations may not be a great place to live. Living in a place long term and vacationing there are two different things. When you vacationed, you never had to do daily things like go shopping, banking, and maintain the place. My advice would be, if you really think you want to buy a place in a vacation resort, rent or lease for a long term first. That is; spend a whole season there or at least a month to really find out what it is like. On a long term vacation, you will need to interact with the people more intimately. You may find there are great people there or you might not like the atmosphere at all.

If it is a beach community you seek, get in touch with a local realtor and lease a place for a whole summer. This is living there and what it would really be like if you bought into the community. Then go. Become part of the community for three months. Learn the local hang outs. Go grocery-shopping and all those other mundane things you have to do to survive. This does two things. First, you find out if you really want to spend that much time there and second, you get an intimate look at the community. At the end of three months you will know what you want to do and you will probably have learned where and what you want to buy, or not. The question is; do you really want to vacation in this same spot every year?

We are beach people and have talked about having a place at the beach. We have decided on the motor home instead because now we can travel to all the beaches and it is always in "vacation" mode. That is; we are tourists. We can act like tourists and enjoy ourselves like tourists. We can go everywhere and for us, that is the lifestyle we want to have. Today, I am sitting in my motor home outside Bryce Canyon National Park. We have been here for two days and have enjoyed ourselves very much. But, in a few hours we will pack up and move a bit to the south to Zion National Park and another adventure will be underway. One adventure leading into the next; we're going to need a rest when this is over.

During the winter of 2019, we stayed for a month in Delray Beach, Florida. When we go to Florida during the winter months, we travel from place to place never staying more than four or five days in any one place. Circumstances lead us to try Delray for the month of March and we loved it. I don't know if we'll do it again or we just might find another place for a month. Time will tell.

Chapter 4: How Do You Feel Today?
Taking care of yourself

There is one thing that you cannot fully control in your retirement and that is your health. Oh, you can do many things to help yourself in this regard, but all in all the fact of your health is a crap shoot. We can all get sick at any time and no matter the prevention measures we take, suddenly we can find ourselves in poor health and unable to do the things we want. But at this moment that is not true, so get moving. Tomorrow is promised to no one. Putting off until next year or next month what you can plan and do today is a recipe for failure.

As we age, there is no kidding ourselves that we do slow down. Our muscles get a bit weaker and our energy levels drop. There is no denying that today is your best day...tomorrow will be a little bit worse and no amount of rehab will change it. But there is no need to despair. No reason to carefully select a tall bridge to end it all...there is plenty left. Just realize that you need to get to it...NOW!

I wrote before about having a life plan going into your retirement. I talked about being paralyzed by all of this freedom. It can happen and you need to be on guard. I spoke with three gentlemen in a campground just yesterday that have different plans. One is on his way to volunteer in a state park. One is traveling with his grandson and one has no plan but to keep going on his adventure that has little structure, but to follow the seasons and keep on going and going and going...like the Energizer Bunny. We all have a different idea of adventure, but the point is to find yours and set sail. Today's plan is not the final plan. It can be changed at any time, being proactive about what you want to do with your life/retirement is a full time job.

All of these people I spoke of are traveling in motor homes or trailers and are anxious to share their stories and adventures. No matter the plan, or lack of one, they're on the move and that is the best health advice I can give. Keep going. Don't become sedentary. Live your life, don't let it live you or you are just waiting around for it to end. If you live by your limitations, they will rule you. Fight back. Fighting back is taking advantage of every day and feeling good about what you are doing. If you're not there, give some serious consideration to changing course, you will be happier and healthier.

We travel in a motor home and the three gentlemen I mentioned above were also in RV's. One was in a trailer with his grandson pulled by his truck, one in a motor home with his wife, and another in a motor home traveling alone. One of the motor homes was new, but the other was not. My own unit is a 2003 (Now a 2012)...we bought it used and have had it for six years. I mention this because travel does not have to be first class airways to an ultimate, all inclusive, resort to be enjoyable. To tell you the truth, the older I get the more I want to sleep in my own bed and eat the food that I prepare. I like to go out to eat, but it's usually too rich and there's too much of it. The real point is I can go where I want and spend less than being at home...and that includes the gas for the motor home!

Since the original writing, we have updated our RV to a 2012 Fleetwood Bounder. Yes, another gently used vehicle. The advantage to buying used in this market is mostly price. The drop off in RV price after a couple of years is substantial. So you can have the latest thing...sort of...at a bargain price buying used. In the first five years of our retirement, we worked our motor home pretty hard, so it was time to renew.

The second advantage to buying used is that most of the bugs are out of the unit. This was not entirely true of our latest unit due mostly to poor dealer prep, but also to equally inadequate manufacturing processes. This is a plague permeating the industry as it strives for maximum profit. With any motor home, you need to make modifications to make it work for you. Sorry to say, there is no perfect unit out there no matter how much you pay.

You do not have to be traveling the world to be active in your retirement. When you are at home, having something to do every day is a good thing. Even if you are not busy all day, accomplishing some tasks will keep you going strong. When I have something to do, it is a reason to get out of bed; a reason to get excited about the day and to stimulate your emotions. It doesn't take a lot to stimulate my emotions these days...but every little bit helps.

Taking care of your health is an important thing in life, but you can't let it run you. Remember, even doctors are running a business. The more they get you into the office, the more money they make. The more tests they run; the more money they make. The more referrals they make; the more referrals are made to them; that's right; and the more money they make. Many retired and non-retired people accept what the doctors give them for appointments. This cuts into my travel time and interrupts my leisure. I'm not having that.

I like to "cluster" my doctor's appointments. That is; get them all done in the same week or even on the same day if possible. I once set a personal best by making three appointments on the same day and keeping them all. This also showed me that there was a lot of duplication of services...such as in-house tests. One of the doctors had already done an EKG on me that day...so the others could not because the insurance would not pay for it. Another thing...blood tests.

There is no need to get an individual blood test for each doctor. If you cluster your appointments, the first doctor will request blood tests for the next visit. This is done on a blood test check-off sheet which is essentially a prescription for the tests. The next doctor will also want blood tests. When you go to that appointment, bring the first blood test sheet and ask him/her to put their requested blood tests on the same sheet; frequently they are the same tests. Also, the second doctor must add his/her name to the sheet so that the results will be sent to them. Most blood test clinics will happily send the results to multiple doctors. Then, do the same thing with the next doctor. If you stay in the same network, this can be automatic.

This accomplishes two things, 1. You go for fewer blood tests, and 2, all the doctors see the results of all your blood tests and know which other doctors you are seeing. Violà...coordinated care for you...a beautiful thing and you control when it happens. When the doctor says your next appointment is on the 27th at 3:00 pm...No, that won't work for me do you have something on the 30th at around 9:00am? They will gladly accommodate...remember they are doctors, but you are the customer and they are running a business.

But don't make doing other things an excuse not to see doctors regularly. Regular care is important to keep medications balanced and keep a close eye on developing conditions. This will keep you healthy…you're already wealthy and wise.

Chapter 5: Forgiving Yourself

Yes, you do deserve it.

I am amazed every day that I don't have to go to work. The fact that I do not answer to someone else for the things I do leaves me smiling. I also gasp unbelievingly that every month, five deposits show up in my checkbook giving me cash to spend and live on. In my mind, especially at first, I really had a hard time realizing that this situation was real and that it would continue for as long as I lived. I still sit in wonder thinking how did I get to this point in my life?

We have friends that live in Florida. They live in one of those over 55, Del Webb type communities. The place is gorgeous with about everything they could ask for. There is a golf course, community center, gym, activity building, etc. all located in a great climate. I was sitting with the gentleman who had worked and saved for his retirement as we all do enjoying the view from his patio overlooking the sixth fairway. He turned to me and simply said, "I guess we did all right." And that about sums it up, don't you think?

I started working in a grocery store when I was sixteen. It was the only part-time job I would ever have. Except for a two-week period between jobs before I was married, I was never unemployed except by choice. That choice was when I went back to college for a year to complete my teaching degree. By the way, college is really a blast. It is wasted on the young and I very much regret not going to college when I was eighteen. Life would have been much easier and not such a grind in the work world had I attained my degree earlier.

So, I worked all of my adult life. Left every morning and came back every evening; sometimes very late. There was that stint where I worked second and third shifts which were nice for my work life, but hell on my family life. But every day...get up...go to work...come home. I'm not different from many others of my generation. We have all worked hard, but did we all prepare for the future? That concerns me...many worked very hard and I fear have very little to show for it or look forward to. Pinch me now. I get up and...do what I want and still get paid for it.

Many things in life are about the choices and decisions we make. The choices we make determine the outcome; more often than not. I once made a choice to leave a good job with a local office machine repair company. It's not that the job was bad or I didn't like it, it was just that I needed the opportunity to work overtime and increase my take home pay and there was no way to do it in my present position. I tried to make a deal with the owner to rearrange my work situation, but we could not reach an agreement. That change worked out well for me; as the owner of the small company sold the business after a short while and the whole thing folded up. That part was a bit of luck.

I also left a job with the federal government after ten years because I saw no way to further advance my career in my present circumstance. This was a bit of a chance because I had to quit my job and return to school for a year in the hopes of landing a new job sometime in the future. The schooling part went great and I did land a job within a few months of finishing, but it was not entirely of my own doing. The city I wanted to work for offered a one-time golden parachute to senior employees. Many took the offer and that left a great number of job openings for me and several others seeking employment. That was a bit of luck but…as a supervisor once told me, "Always be ready for your next promotion." Thanks for that advice Bob. I was ready and when opportunity presented itself…sometimes you're just in the right place at the right time, but you have to put yourself in that favorable position. Many don't understand that and end up lamenting lost opportunities when they only have themselves to blame. The most society gives you is opportunity; you have to seize it.

I could have retired from the federal government at 57 years old had I continued working there. In making this job change however; I would have summers off and much more time to spend with my family. I thought that the 20 or so summers I would have off would equal the three more years I would have to work, so it was a wash. It turned out to be even better than that.

During my work life, I was always a "pay yourself first" saver. But after I changed careers at 40 years old, I began to seriously think of retirement…remember, I promised myself that I would retire at 60…and I set my savings goals to meet that retirement date. Once I latched on to the concept of the "ballpark" nest egg figure for savings, I went at it earnestly; more on the "ballpark figure" later and how to find yours. For now let's just say it is your financial goal for retirement savings to maintain your present lifestyle. So, I have no problem forgiving myself. I can wake up every morning and fall asleep every night with a clear conscience. I took nothing that was not deserved and I feel I always gave more than was asked.

Are there some things I would have done differently? You bet. A Monday morning quarterback always plays a perfect game. That is, if you already know the ending, perfect decisions are easy. The tough part is making decisions while the game is going on. So, yes; I would have done some things differently, but those are the decisions I made...this is how it turned out...and as Pat says..."It is what it is."

There is nothing I can go back and change. I can admit to myself when I was wrong and I can applaud the good things I've done. This is satisfaction and no amount of regret can change what happened. So, deal with it. You have what you have and as they say, you made your own bed.

There were times when I was lucky and things turned out right. Sometimes it was a struggle and I had to work through it. There are adjustments/decisions that you make as you go through life and at some point you enter your second phase.

The second phase, your retirement, is where you call all of the shots. You are no longer working for the money, but the money is working for you. I read about many people that start a business in their retirement. The business is profitable, but many of them not wildly so and they don't have to be. The satisfaction is in the doing and the capital that they saved for their retirement; financed the dream of owning their own business. The profit is just icing on the cake.

The point about money in retirement is how you look at it. Money, especially money you have saved, is something to be put to work; not to spend. As an example, if you have $10 in your pocket, that is cash to spend. But, if you have $1000, that is money to be put to work and the $10 that you make from it (in interest or profit), is the money you spend...and you still have the $1000. See the difference? And next month, you get another $10 to spend and you still have the original $1000...and that goes on forever.

So, there you are with your cup of coffee, reading the morning paper at 5:30 AM...yes, 5:30 because now you get up because you want to, because the day is yours...you sip your coffee and you contemplate, "How did I get here?" The answer is: you got here through hard work and perseverance and you don't have to apologize to anyone. You are what you are and "That's the way it is." So, you put that $10 in your pocket and you go to breakfast with your buddies smiling all the way.

Chapter 6: Spouses and Beliefs

Can you spell c-o-m-p-a-t-a-b-l-e?

Ah! The moment you know you are in love. That feeling...the heart pounding high...the stirring...the desire...alright, cool it. OK, so after that, what? As wonderful as that life–long love is in the beginning, a real relationship that lasts into retirement takes some work and mutual understanding. No more does this become evident then when you do retire. Its 24-7 togetherness, baby...can you take it?

I described earlier our first few months of retirement. As compatible as I thought we were and the plans we had made and the understandings I thought we had...bam! Life happens. Compatibility starts way before that and the lack of compromise, I think, is the undoing of many a relationship.

After the glow fades a bit, there is living life together day after day. The little compromises, made almost continuously, are the building blocks in a marriage. No two relationships look the same. Often they do not even make sense to those looking from the outside. One thing everybody knows though, when you see a good relationship, you can feel it, but you can't deconstruct it and reassemble it as your own.

You can't say it's 50/50, but you can't keep score because you don't know the rules. Only those in the relationship know the rules and they probably couldn't articulate them very well. It's built over time...that's what is real. That's why you can't judge or imitate. Other couples can observe and even try to copy, but it can't work unless those agreements; some stated, some not are made over time.

Back to the fading glow…not so much that it fades, but it changes. The physical relationship with its fireworks and earth moving…well…we move on. We start living together and becoming one out of two that are still two. There's a big thing. Individualism is maintained in good relationships. There is the couple…together…and there are two people that each have a life. There has to be time and allowances for both or you will strangle each other both literally and figuratively.

And so you approach retirement, and the kids are grown and gone,…If you are defined so much by what you do for work that there is only that and you as a couple with your spouse…there could be a problem here because the "work" you and that identity is going to disappear. If all that is left is the "you" identified as a couple…that is a real problem. That is why you need to identify yourself as an individual without work after retirement before you actually do retire. That second phase is important to identifying you…after the work you. Once I found the website "My Second Phase," I took the surveys and identified some of the things I would like to do. It's important that you put some time into this. You don't have to use this specific site, but find a guide somewhere. It is important for your retirement, your relationship, and the meaning of your life. It is the reason some people are bored with retirement and other people thrive.

Actually, I wish I had found "My Second Phase" during my work life. It would have helped me be less work centric and more of a well rounded person. I would have known myself much better and I think it would have made me a happier person.

AARP now offers a website called "Life Re-imagined." This website provides information about retirement and planning for it. Don't feel that you are too young to look at this and consider what it means for you. A couple plans financially over 40 years for a successful retirement. Why not consider how and what you are going to do in retirement, long before you get there? There is a reason AARP solicits people that are only 50 years old. By that time most people should be considering very seriously what they are going to do in their retirement years whether that is ten, twenty or twenty-five years down the road.

Finding that meaning in your second phase makes you anxious to get on with it. Once I found it, I couldn't wait to retire. I couldn't wait to start doing those things I had found were important to me. I had become so wrapped up in production at work that I had lost time to be creative. Creativity is what makes me tick and I couldn't wait to get the time and the freedom to get the creative juices flowing again. Once it happened, I couldn't remember what it was like to work and I didn't want to go back.

I think many people go back to work or can't retire because they never get to this point. What they do defines what they are and they can't let it go or there just isn't anything else to go to. Other than that, some people just can't give up the paycheck fearing that they will run out of money, but that is another chapter and we'll get to that.

In retirement with now having the time to be creative, I took my music to a new place where I had never been. I started writing songs that were important and most people say are good music. I met another retiree that had set up a digital recording studio in his bonus room and I complemented his dreams. He was producing his own music and wanted to help others produce theirs. Together we have done some very good things. I have finished and released an album of my own music. I never thought I would say that. It's unbelievably exciting.

I also began to write. The first edition of this book was my first attempt. This edition is my ninth. I have also written six novels: The Reggie Slater Mystery Series *Bethany Blues, Ocean City Blues, Key West Blues,* and The Russ Deever Mystery Series *Beach Blues, Carousel Blues, and Marginal Blues.* The books were an absolute blast to write and I think I will continue to write until I can't do it anymore. I write more than I play music, but I find both fulfilling and enjoyable.

Getting the books published is now possible on your own; there is little to hold you back. There are plenty of web sites where you can do it yourself or ask for assistance. For me, Amazon and the Kindle was a natural match. The upload is easy and your book as you wrote it is on sale the same day. Unbelievable!

Once your mind is freed from the shackles of what you must do at work, your brain can create music and prose that you can share. What a great and rewarding feeling. This first edition of this book alone has been downloaded over 800 times. That gives me great satisfaction that I can share my ideas with so many people and help them to attain success in their second phase.

The finances and the planning give you the financial independence to do whatever you desire or are capable of in retirement. That is the secret to retirement happiness. That is why it is so important to find your own niche of happiness. Finding what that is, is not an easy task and requires some soul searching. It takes you beyond the "work" that defined you and more towards the real you. Scary stuff...we're talking a lot of introspection here...maybe more than you ever have done before. It can be a little disconcerting what you find down that rabbit hole, Alice.

Anyway, back to living with your spouse after retirement. If you both discover what the individual "you" is before or early in your retirement years, now you have pursuits, dreams, and things you want to do on an individual basis. You must give each other the independence required to pursue those dreams. But, part of that dream must always be reserved for the two of you together.

I would hope I've impressed upon you enough that conversations have to take place about what you want to do as a couple after your retirement. Day to day, and long-term vacations and outings are the stuff of great times and memories together. It's almost like going back to the courtship days...a forever honeymoon, without the fireworks and the earth moving stuff...careful, you might throw out a hip!

Chapter 7: Responsibilities

Things you have to do vs. Things you want to do

During your work life, there were several responsibilities tugging at you from a myriad of directions. There was also a jumble of priorities that included work as well as home, family, relatives, etc. We seemed to manage all of these as a group of juggling cats and the convenient response if you could not was, "I have to work." This got you "out of" some things that were not all that important. No one ever challenged that because that block of time was your livelihood. But now that excuse is gone and people figure you're retired now so you have time to do whatever they ask. Not, so fast. No, you don't!

Part of the joy of retirement is spontaneity. That joyous gift of doing what strikes you at the moment. If you over schedule your life as it was when you worked, that joy is erased. Make sure you stay in control of your time. Learn to say no...not for any reason other than you don't want to.

We love our grandchildren, but we did not want to raise them. It is difficult these days for families with both parents working to make ends meet financially and bear the cost of day-care for their children, your grandchildren. I understand that they need two incomes especially to feed that immediate reward syndrome they seem to have developed, but anyway, we will help out all we can when we are home and that is without reservation, but not every day. We help with day care as we are available, but altering travel plans is off the table. We will take responsibility, but we do not want to own the responsibility of caring for those precious kids every day...they are ours to spoil and we practice it well.

We have friends that fell into the raising of their grandchildren trap. Her motivations were golden and well meaning and her grandchildren love her, but her husband finally retired and she continued to care for the children daily. He wanted to travel, she had become too attached. A few years after his retirement, he died. They never traveled together. Now she travels alone.

Travel is not the burden being away from home that it once was. We are not Lewis & Clark traveling the Missouri in our canoe out of touch for months at a time. Our journeys do not take us far from civilization and we don't have to hewn our own canoes. All states and cities have airports…even Canada…so we are no more than a day away if we must return home for any reason. With cell phones and Skype we are always in touch. It works for us when we miss our kids and grandkids as I'm sure it does for all of them.

Bill paying while on the road has become automatic. Accounts can be set up through your bank or utility company to have appropriate amounts deducted directly from your checking account. All of this can be closely monitored by email. It really is a snap and anyone can do it. As a hint: direct pay to your utilities and such works much better than having your bank cut a check and send it. Direct pay is also without fee and your bills don't have to be paid ahead of time. The entire process can be double-checked by monitoring your bank accounts on-line.

We will most likely never sell our home because our extended family lives in the area. We will always return because that is where our hearts are. But travel, yes we must, but we never stray so far that the strings of our hearts are not still attached.

There are still tasks we must perform on our house. "Never stop improving..." isn't that the motto. Our house requires maintenance and updating as do all homes. Now that we are retired, we have time to perform some of these tasks that we have planned for years to make our property better and more livable. This is that place we raised our children, but now it is just ours, and the grandchildren's when they visit, so it has been transformed to perform those functions. It is always a work in progress as they say, but at some point the changing will be done and maintenance will be our task between trips. And, finally, when the trip taking is done it will be the place we are at peace with our lives.

As the years pass, I am surely capable of doing some major improvements, but do I want to? A major project requires three things: money, time, and effort. There was a time when we had little money, little time, but plenty of energy to get the task done. I/we did most of the routine and improvement work on the house. Things sure have changed. Now there is more money, surprisingly not as much time, and the energy available diminishes with each passing day. So, we made some changes in how things get done.

Because there is an increase in funds available, we can hire someone to get some things done. This solves the time problem and the lack of energy. More than one thing gets done at once and there is more time to enjoy what we have had done and time is freed up for traveling. It's a win-win situation. Sometimes you just have to give in.

And there are the mundane tasks to be performed for everyday living: shopping, cooking, cleaning and the like all need to still get done. These all take a little bit longer as the years go by so we have to leave time for them. The doctor's visits and blood tests along with leisure activities, such as: movies, side trips, and just cool things to do…like breakfast or lunch with friends.

It's a grand life and you have to make time for it. Don't fall into the trap of having it planned for you like your work life was. You got over that and got out. This is your reward time. Don't give it away a little piece at a time.

I have spoken of volunteer work and things that fill your time and fulfill you…you deserve all of them without standing in line…so get up and get going…and don't forget to ask for your senior discount…and don't feel bad if the teenager behind the counter doesn't ask to see your ID…you've earned the discount with every one of those wrinkles.

Chapter 8: You Don't Work...You Have Time
Or do you?

Oh, how many times have I heard this? Now that you are retired, you should be able to respond to any demand on your time; right? You no longer have to respond to an alarm clock, trudge off to work, come home, do chores or more work, go to bed, and get up to do it all again the next day. No one would ask you to do extra things then. After all, you had to work. Your life was organized around that work schedule and it was all neat and tidy.

Now you don't work. You are free and everyone thinks that you don't have anything to do. They want to help you out with that and start placing demands on your time. And you don't really mind because after all, you don't work and you have the time. But there is no longer an organizing factor to your day. There is no work schedule to plan around. You have the organization of an independent contractor with ten jobs going all at once...trying to keep all of your customers satisfied. It becomes like watching a three-ring circus. You just can't keep your attention focused.

As this situation develops, you realize you are spread too thin. You over-volunteered or in some way over committed your time. I found myself keeping a plan book as I did when I worked. How could this happen?

Looking back, it's not hard to see how it happened. All of the maintenance you have been putting off doing on your property, now becomes a high priority and screams at you every day to get it done. There are those organizations that you have committed to help; you are now serious about that. There are visits to parents and doctors appointments. And oh, yes you are retired and you want to do some fun things which now it seems you have to schedule and actually feel a bit guilty about the things you are not getting done. Your days become filled with commitments in a disorganized way and you realize that it really is out of control. And you don't even work. How did you get it all done then?

The answer is; you didn't. What you did do was compartmentalize. If you had a nine to five work schedule, those hours were sacred and committed. Evening hours were for getting the essentials done at home. Weekends were yard work or property maintenance. Meetings for volunteer work were relegated to an evening or two per month. It was all very neat and tidy. Don't forget, your energy level was much higher and you were younger then.

I'm sure this is not a phenomenon that just happened to me, but surely happens to all retirees. The solution lies in getting organized and paring those things that are not as important to you. In organizing, I have previously mentioned clustering your health appointments. Don't scatter them around and just accept the time and day an appointment is offered. Schedule them at times that are convenient to you and reschedule them if you must.

Also, your commitments to organizations need to be realistic and not confine your activities. It's all well and good to volunteer your time, but that is supposed to be free time. Your commitments shouldn't cause you to not schedule activities with your spouse or friends. Leave time for you. That is what retirement is all about.

Grandchildren and family are tougher still. Some things you want to do and some things you need to do. Caring for elderly parents certainly falls into the latter category and grandkids can fall into both. Just try not to become the caregivers to your grandchildren and become indispensible. Your retirement, or at least much of it, is supposed to be for you. The pull of grandchildren...the wish to be part of their lives...is strong and certainly limits the duration of our travel time. Seems that about six to eight weeks is the limit and then we must return to reengage.

The key here, and this is imperative, is to carve out blocks of time for your retirement together. Give time to your charities, to your parents, to your health but leave time for each other and yourself. Time to travel is important and that means scheduling so that there are large blocks of time that you can disengage from responsibilities. It surely is different for everyone, but it takes some thought and planning to be successful. If you over commit in the beginning, it is more difficult to disengage.

I mentioned at the beginning of this writing that retirement took planning to be successful; not only financial planning, but personal planning as well. It would be natural to experiment with a few volunteer possibilities, dive into a few of your passions now that you have the freedom to do so. It is easy to get overextended in your exuberance. You should be prepared to jettison those things that do not satisfy or fulfill the goals that satisfy your passions.

Contemplate this scenario. You volunteer for a cause or get appointed to the board of an organization. Usually this requires that you attend one board meeting per month. Sure you can do that. Oh, but it doesn't end there. Then there is committee work. After all, if you're going to serve on a board, you have to serve on a committee and it makes sense that you are asked to or volunteer for a committee that fits your passion. All great; right? Well, of course there's work to be done on that committee which requires getting involved with other members or the organization's workers. You want to do a good job so you dive right in.

You go to the board meeting. You go to the committee meeting. You work with other committee members. You interact with the organization....you get the idea. After awhile that one meeting per month is turning into a job. Maybe you did this with two organizations trying to fill your time. Along with your home chores, yard work, and maybe some travel sprinkled in, you find yourself overextended.

Some choices will have to be made. How much passion and energy do you have? What do you really want to focus on? Yes, you are going to have to have a real sit down with yourself to make some decisions. Do it and do it soon. I don't say to up and quit. That's probably just not in your nature. I would suggest letting your term run out and focusing on the things that are most important to you.

The problem with retirement is that you have freedom like you have never experienced before in your life. Your mind becomes free to contemplate possibilities for your time and your passion. You begin to dabble and find that you have many talents. You also find that there are many avenues to develop those talents. In your ambition, you need to temper your drive to do it all and focus. Dabble at will...because it is great fun to experiment, but do so with the mindset that at some point a decision will have to made whether to continue or cut your losses and take a different path. You can learn to play the piano for your own enjoyment or you can become a concert pianist or something in between. Only you can decide when you are satisfied or detect when your spouse has heard enough of you practicing your scales.

Chapter 9: Retirement Finances
Who's Your Daddy Now?

We have talked about being mentally and emotionally ready for retirement. All that is fine, but you need to be able to afford what you want to do and to pay your bills during the retirement years. To be emotionally comfortable, you need to have enough money so that you do not spend your time worrying about it. You surely need to keep paying attention to your financial situation, but to be at peace enough to take advantage of your dreams; you need to be comfortable with your finances.

During retirement, you reap what you have sown. I'm not purporting to be some financial genius because I have an income stream that is more than adequate for us in retirement, but I'm here. I didn't start saving from the first dollar I made or go around in a sack cloth; although we were pretty frugal or should I say not extravagant and I think most importantly, we didn't have to have everything right now. We had what we needed and then some. We bought what we could afford and never got in over our heads. I guess you could say we lived just a bit below our means. And now, the money rolls in every month and it's enough. So, how can you do it too without so much of the hype that you hear or read? All it takes is diligence and paying attention.

First, at some point in your life, preferably in your late thirties or early forties or before; give your retirement some serious thought. By some thought, I mean make some sort of outline of a plan and set some modest goals for your retirement. Make sure you are taking advantage of what is offered by your company. If you are with a company that offers a savings match in some sort of 401k retirement plan and you're not taking full advantage of it, do it. If you are not with a company that offers anything, it's time to think about maybe changing your situation and getting with a company that does. If you are with someone that offers a plan, what will the payout look like when you are retirement age? And what age would that be? If you don't know, find out. If your company doesn't offer a plan that's not catastrophic but, you will need to make your own. If your company does offer a plan, it may not be enough and you need to make your own anyway to make up the difference. We'll get to how you know and how you would do that in a minute.

I fear that these days most of the generation that follows me will have to make their own retirement fund from the very start. That's OK, but they can't put it off. They need to do it and do it soon. Without any type of prodding or mandatory deduction, most young people go for the cash to spend now, not the savings. That's a natural instinct and it was true for my generation as well. But many in my generation were forced to contribute to retirement programs by their unions, their companies, or governments.   You can argue if that was a good or bad thing, but at least it got us started.

Lately, a couple of items in the USA Today caught my eye. One was that most middle-class Americans believe that saving $250K for retirement is what they will need. If we break down that thinking; if 4% per year is what retirees should withdraw from their retirement savings in order for those savings to last 30 years, means that most of middle class America believes that $10,000 per year or $833 per month or

$192 per week is enough to sustain them in retirement along with their Social Security. I don't think so!

Also, I read that Social Security retirees are getting a 1.7% raise this year. That is a good thing, but it means that the average couple will be receiving $26,112 per year or $2,176 per month or $502 per week from Uncle Sam. Do they believe that this is enough? Well, adding the two together means that middle class America will be receiving $36,112 per year or $3009 per month or $694 per week to sustain them in their retirement. A couple might be able to live in a small apartment, drive a 1999 Toyota Corolla, and pay their bills, but not much else.

Now, I'm more than a little concerned about what the future holds for these retirees. A couple can barely sustain themselves on about $3,000 per month. Food, shelter, and utilities will eat that up in a hurry. Other than sitting at home watching basic cable, that income will not make for an active retirement. I'm hoping that many misunderstood the question and thought they had to independently save that much and save as much or more in plans offered at work. I also think that I'm being overly optimistic.

So, if this is an average...some people are saving more and just as many are saving less. Scary thought isn't it? With this type of income, many retirees will be looking not for a few niceties, but rather necessities from their government...that is the rest of us. The message has to be delivered that more needs to be saved for retirement, it's not that hard, and everybody can and must do it to take care of themselves and not expect big government, which is the rest of us, to support them.

Without encouragement from company savings plans or pensions, I fear that many will wait too long to begin their retirement savings program and then get caught short or worse have to keep on working long after they should or want to retire. If you're young and don't understand "should" or "want to" retire, just hold on, it will come to you, eventually. If you are reading this, it is starting to come to you already.

One of the problems is that it seems that a nest egg for retirement is a huge amount of money to save. "Save Your Million" the articles across the financial pages read. "How to Grow a 7-figure Nest Egg" we all want to know. Wow! It seems like so much that most people don't even know where or how to start. They are stalled by the enormity of the task. The answer is to start...yes, start small. Start with five-dollars a week if you must, but start and start young, if you can.

The first step needed to begin planning for retirement is the knowledge of what you have now. That is the starting place to calculate what your total retirement income will look like when you reach retirement age. Oh, there's a big question. What is your retirement age? Let's talk about that first and then discuss how much you need to save for retirement because in this case "age matters." The calculation is very dependent on the number of years between now and that age due to the "magic" of compound interest.

Well, your retirement age is a decision that is really up to you. Yes, really...your retirement age is your decision. Your retirement date surely affects your plan and you need to be a really aggressive saver to retire early, but it's still up to you. I decided that when I changed careers at 39 years old that I would retire at 60. Why 60? Well, remember I was in a government job that would have let me retire at 57 years old, but I didn't want to do that job anymore. So, I went back to school, finished my degree, and went into education where I had a better retirement plan…at least one that I liked better…and summers off. I figured that the 2+ months I had off every year would make up for the three extra years I would have to work in my old job so I decided to aim at 60 for a retirement age. Don't get stuck. Take control of your career and your future.

In my mid-thirties, I made that decision to change careers and started working on my degree. There were a few reasons for this, but mostly it was about advancement and there were forces that said I couldn't in my present situation. This is an important thing to realize for your success…the fact that only you are in charge of it. There are always others that try to stipulate what you can and cannot do, but that is not true for anyone. There are those that always say you can't, but you can. Figure out what you need to do to make it happen and work toward that goal. It works with finances and it works with jobs and careers. There are always barriers. Learn not to give in to them.

I don't mean you have to fight all the time and push against authority. One must realize however, that your destiny is in your own hands. Circumstances may work against you, but learn to overcome them. When you work at a job, you are a corporation in that you provide your employer with a service that it desires. For that service the company gives you a wage. You have the right to negotiate that wage. If your employer doesn't want to negotiate or provide you with fair compensation for your work, find another employer. It's a fee for service deal. If work was all that rewarding, people would do it for the pure joy of it. I don't know anyone that gives their paycheck back; except maybe for Donald Trump.

I say aim at a retirement age because like you, I wasn't sure I would be able to afford it. I needed to accumulate a nest egg to supplement my pension if I was to retire early. There was also the matter of health insurance, and 60 years old is well before social security and Medicare kicks in. It was my dream to retire at 60 years of age and I set about making that dream come true for us.

I ran across something in the newspaper that got me rolling. It was called the "Ballpark Estimate." I still have it and I share it with my friends. It listed everything you own, owe, and expect as income in retirement all in about the four inch by 12 inch document. Using the numbers that were entered, it led you to estimate how much money you would need in retirement every month/year. From this, you could see if you would have enough saved by the time you retired; if you did, great. If you didn't...which I didn't...you have to make plans about how to make up the deficit by the retirement age you selected or picked a later date.

I stuck with the 60 year old date I stated earlier for retirement. Then I went about making a plan to make up the funds that the "Ballpark Estimate" showed I was lacking. You can find this worksheet "on-line" by searching "Ballpark Estimate."

So, armed with this meager, admittedly rough estimate, I began my investment life. I invested first in a stock fund and then a few stocks. One or two at first, but always for the long-term in something called a dividend reinvestment plan. This is a "set it and forget it" type of investment. You invest a lump sum, say $3,000 and $100 per month automatically deducted from your checking account. That $100 purchases more shares. Oh, I felt the pinch at first, but as I got raises, I didn't feel it so much. And then I started another when I could afford it, and another, until I had about eight diversified stocks and funds growing all the time using my $100 per month contribution and dividends paid by the stocks bought even more. These dividend reinvestment plans can be started for a few dollars directly with companies. A list of companies offering these plans can be found "on-line" by searching "Dividend Reinvestment Plans."

I have never had a broker, but that's not to say I was a blind investor. I read a lot. I have had a subscription to *Money* since it was a newsletter. I read business publications, newsletters, and yes the business section in the newspaper. I read and take the advice of those who provide sound and realistic thinking. I always want to know if I am on the right track. As an example, I was reading an ad about a very successful investment fund. It showed what stocks were in the fund by category and how much of each stock was owned by percentage. I compared that to my own portfolio and realized that I was missing a sector. I found out which stocks listed offered dividend reinvestment plans, decided on one, and added it to my own portfolio. That investment has really paid off. It is an energy stock and those stocks do well in tough times. It has kept my portfolio growing, even during times of poor market performance.

And there was one small piece of luck in my stock portfolio. I once worked for a major corporation in my younger days that had a retirement plan with employee contributions. I contributed a small portion of my pay, I think 4%, I/we didn't have much money at the time, a young family, and my wife was home raising the kids and not working. I only stayed with the company for about three years but when I left, they gave me back what I had contributed and that included some cash and some company stock...I think about 69 shares if I remember. That stock has split several times to the point I now own over 1,100 shares and they are worth more than $180 each. Yeah, it's a lot of money. I suppose this is a lesson in starting investing when you are young because time is money, but this is the only stock I owned until I was about 35 years old.

This stock is not a dividend reinvestment plan. A check was sent to my home every quarter as a dividend. This was a big deal for a young family because it was like a gift in the mail and usually meant a dinner out for us. So, there was my bit of luck in the investing world that is paying much higher dividends today and helping to finance my retirement. That quarterly check is now part of my retirement pay.

The other problem I saw about retiring at 60 years old was health care. Medicare kicks in at 65 years old, but what was I and my spouse going to do for health care from 60 to 65, I would have to finance it myself and that would be expensive. Teachers cannot have traditional IRA's because they have a retirement plan (to which they contribute heavily) but they can have what is called a 403b plan which is about the same thing. It is before tax money removed from your pay and invested. This can later be turned into an annuity or taken as a lump sum after age 59 ½. I opened one of these with a guaranteed 4% return and for many years earned much more than that. That

4% looks pretty good right now. I still have it because I never did need that money for health care costs. That was another bit of luck but I kind of used it for another purpose which you can read in a later chapter as "My Big Mistake."

When Pat and I retired at 60 years old, three months apart, a wonderful thing had happened over the years. I was in the National Guard until 1993 and retired with 21 years military service. When I left, there were minimal benefits that only kicked in at age 60. There was a small pension that I calculated as retirement income in my Ballpark Estimate and some travel benefits. But as the world political situation heated up in the 1990's and the Guard was called more and more into active service, National Guard retirees were granted many of the benefits of full-time service members and one of those was health care in retirement. Retirement for a National Guard member begins at age sixty.

So, there was my piece of luck concerning health care for myself and Pat. For about $45 per month, Pat and I received full health care from TriCare between the ages of 60 and 65. We went to a nearby Navy clinic and loved it. Our prescription coverage was included also. My National Guard investment has paid off in a big way. Because I had a draft number of 7, that's right 7, I would have surely been drafted, I joined the National Guard and after 21 years ended up with a pension and inexpensive health care...turns out to be one of the best investments I ever made.

As we are now over 65 years old, we have joined Medicare. The TriCare coverage is still in effect, but in a different way. We pay for our Medicare as everyone else does, but we do not have to buy supplemental insurance or a prescription drug plan. TriCare for Life which has no premium now acts as our supplemental and drug care coverage.

I would be negligent and in big trouble if I listed only the above as my benefits of joining the Air National Guard. I learned many great skills in the guard and even worked for them full-time for ten years, but those were still small benefits compared to the biggest benefit of all. Let me explain...

During my National Guard training, I was assigned to Chanute Air Force Base in Illinois. The on-base church sponsored a program to "entertain" the local college girls and the young men in training at the base. One day, a bus load of girls came to the base and about 20 young men, including me, got on the bus and each of us sat next to a girl. The girls, being the clever college coeds that they were, had separated one to a seat so that a young man had to sit next to them. I sat next to a pretty young blond girl who is now my wife...true story. The bus driver was my best man two years later...I kid you not.

As most people do, as a young family man I carried a healthy amount of life insurance. I tried the whole life model at first, but found that not to be the money maker it was sold to be. So, eventually I discontinued that and bought term life and invested the rest. Term life is much cheaper than whole life so it is a better buy. If you want savings, it is best to invest the rest in something else. So, I did.

Life insurance is a bet between you and the insurance company. You bet you are going to die...the insurance company bets that you won't. Your bet covers the future for your wife and kids, the insurance company makes money with the money you give them. According to the actuary tables...the insurance company always wins. So if you no longer need to play...that is you no longer have need for the big dollars protection...get out of the game and cancel your life insurance or at least most of it.

You buy enough life insurance to protect the future in case you won't be around. When you are younger...the concern is your wife and kids...covering your lost income if you die and your kid's college education and such. Once the kids are grown and you are nearing retirement, that need is gone. Then you can reduce your insurance needs to covering your funeral costs and final expenses...this greatly reduces your premiums. This is another way to save in/for retirement.

So, how do you finance your retirement? Find a job you like that provides you with fair compensation. Make a plan for how much money you need to retire. Invest, save, and manipulate your income and benefits so that you can retire with benefits and income to provide you with enough in your retirement. Sounds simple enough, doesn't it? It is, but it takes attention...your attention. Your attention to adjust your spending and investments, constant goal setting, and a dose of good luck as you review and plan every year recreating a plan to keep yourself on track.

I recently read an article where Janet Yellen (former Fed Chief) said that three things are necessary for economic success: opportunity, effort, and luck. I believe that is true, but there are some caveats I would add. I believe that opportunity is greatly related to effort. That is, there is opportunity for all, but it is not always handed to you...it isn't even always obvious. It is true that most things are what you make them, but it is more than that. Sometimes opportunity needs to be chased down and wrangled...maybe even hog-tied. Finding out that there is opportunity is often half the battle. To be successful one must chase down the opportunity one wants to create. It is true that some people are handed their opportunity, but most of us must make our own.

So effort plays a big part in seeking out the opportunity to be successful and once you find the opportunity it is the personal effort of the person to gain the skills to take advantage of that opportunity. Many people fall down here...mostly those to whom the opportunity comes easily. OK, you've got it...now what? Get on the horse and ride cowboy or the pack will leave you behind.

Then Ms. Yellen mentions luck. It is not the luck like winning the lottery. The luck I believe she means and the one I think is the most important is the luck you make for yourself and that is also related to effort. If you are in a job and have put great effort into that job and increased your skills...the promotion will go your way...or at least it should...and if it doesn't...keep at it. Increase your skills and make yourself valuable either to that company or to another company that will see your value and offer you the opportunity you deserve.

To attain what you want is up to you. It starts with your effort. Your effort to seek out opportunity; your effort to take advantage of that opportunity; and your effort to be in that position to advance and make your own luck will lead to your success. Yes, it really is true. Good work does pay off. Oh, not always right away, but surely in the long run. If you say this hasn't worked for you, look within because your actions are really all you can control. Is there something else you could have done to make it better?

Enough retirement income...what is *e-n-o-u-g-h*? There are those experts that say to replace your income from your job 100%...some say 80%...some 60%. We can discuss this point for hours on end, but the truth is you can live comfortably on about 60% of your total working income, if you are debt-free going into retirement. Ah! Debt free...how does that happen?

To live comfortably on 60% of your former income in retirement, it is essential that you go into retirement in a debt free state. If you have debt when you retire, you can add the cost of that debt to the 60% which is ok if you have more retirement income, but you may have to delay your retirement to catch up on your debt. Either of these options didn't sit well with me.

Debt free means debt free. No car loans, credit card debt, mortgages, or personal loans or you need more retirement income or to delay your retirement date. How is this possible you say? By just being a little bit frugal and timing your purchases to make sure they are paid off on the day you retire. Remember, you have a plan and a date you are working towards. You are also constantly reviewing that plan and setting incremental goals. That keeps your plan real and on-track.

As far as a mortgage, sure you need a place to live, but when you buy it matters. If you get a 30 year mortgage when you are 35 and you plan to retire at 60, that math doesn't quite work...but, yes it can. If you pay a bit more each month, mortgages can be paid off early...yes, as much as five years. And you accelerate payments at the end when the kids are gone and your expenses are lower. Remember, every year you are doing a financial analysis of your situation, adjusting your goals, always with your eye on the ball of that retirement date. And always think about refinancing when interest rates drop...it is a big saver.

Be modest in your purchases. That Lexus would sure be nice, but what will it cost me in the long run? Does it mean working until I'm 65 instead of 60? Not for me...but I do have some vices that I satisfy. I like convertibles. New ones are nice, but two or three year old ones are half the price and you still get the same thrill as the wind blows through your thinning hair. Just a little compromise can go a long way to being debt free, yet satisfied. Also buying a high level Toyota gets you almost the same vehicle as the Lexus at a greatly reduced price.

Credit cards are a great tool. I use them all the time. Carrying cash is chancy, especially far from home. It is easier to track your spending and be protected from theft with a credit card. But they are a huge temptation. You can always afford whatever is in front of you...just pull out the plastic! Want to curb this entirely? The experts say to only use cash, but that is impractical. Better still; sign up for automatic bill pay so that your entire credit card balance is paid in-full directly from your checking account every month. So that when you are staring at that new wide-screen TV at the electronics store, you know the bill is coming due in a few weeks. Never carry a balance on a credit card...it is more expensive than whatever you are buying.

You may be thinking....does this guy ever finance anything? Of course I do. But I never remove money from my retirement savings be it stocks or cash accounts to do so. Why? Because I am afraid that I will never put it back and then I would be behind on my retirement goals. So, I finance some things like the purchase of my motor home or a car, but I make a plan to pay it off at an accelerated rate.

A motor home is a large purchase, much more than my house! Usually, you are trading one you have for the new(er) one. It works like buying a car. The trouble with new motor homes is that they are very, very expensive. A modest new 30' motor home can easily go for more than $100,000. That sure can put a dent in your retirement savings. So, I don't buy new...like my convertibles...I buy gently used. You have to shop around, but three to four year old motor homes are available for half the price of new with less than 20,000 miles on them. These generally come with several options because motor home owners are a bit anal about adding personal touches to their vehicles. So, you end up with a four year old vehicle loaded with options that you don't have to pay for. When I picked up my 2003 motor home purchase at the dealer in 2007, it was sitting next to a brand new one of the same model and I couldn't tell them apart. The dealer prep of a motor home is a thorough cleaning and tune up inside and out. That motor home was magnificent and I drove it for over six years and traveled all over the country.

We have since purchased a newer motor home than described above. I went to a cut rate dealer because of the price...mistake. The dealer prep was nowhere near as complete as described above and I ended up doing many things myself. Sometimes paying a bit more is really worth it.

So, by buying used you save about half the cost. What about the financing? I have a personal line of credit with my bank that exists with my house (paid off) as collateral. This gets me a mortgage loan rate on anything I use this account to finance. So, if motor home loan rates are going for 8%, I get the money for around 3 to 4%. But there is a danger here. You have to be disciplined. You need to create your own payment schedule. The bank does not tell you what to pay every month and they will accept just the interest payment. I generally make a schedule to pay off the loan in three years or less. I can flex my payments every month to account for holiday expenses and such, but I try to stick to the schedule I created.

And what do I pay for a motor home after all this. Remember, I said a new one costs well over $100,000. I paid $55,000 for the 2003 I had and my trade was worth $20,000 so I financed $35,000 for the vehicle I drove for six years. I cite this purchase as an example of how you can purchase something you want for less, finance it for less, and still enjoy it the most. My newest motor home was not financed at all. I used accumulated savings during my first five years of retirement to finance the purchase. In other words I paid cash. Okay...this guy is still saving money with only his retirement pension? Yes, I am...more on that later.

All of this goal setting is nice and the planning seems not too difficult if you pay attention, but what happens when life happens and you find yourself between a rock and a hard place? What happens when all of a sudden your expenses exceed your income and you can't see any way out?

First, never borrow money from yourself. That is; do not remove money from your stock plans or bank accounts that is part of your retirement savings. Use everything else you have first. That is: checking accounts, emergency savings, etc. and then borrow money from other accounts. Yes, you should always have emergency savings equal to six-months of salary. But never touch your retirement savings because it is unlikely that you will ever put it back and that just delays your retirement date.

My wife and I had made a pledge that we would finance the college education of our two daughters. Their ages are close and that would mean that for two years, they would be in college together. We had saved money for their college and we took advantage of the ten-month payment plan offered by the college. We received some small grants but by and large, because we were a two income family, meant we were shouldering the burden of college tuition without much help. The ten-month plan is good, but I wished we could spread the payments out further and see below how that is possible with some financial manipulation.

For the first two years, it was all right and we were making ends meet and making the college tuition payments. But in the second two years, when they were both in college, things got a little tight and the payments exceeded our means to pay. It turns out that students can borrow money easier and at a better rate than their parents. So, we had each of our daughters take out a student loan which is interest and payment differed until they get out of school. This took some of the pressure off while two were in school, but our everyday savings account went down to less than $900 during that time. The differed loans were later paid off when only the younger one was in school, but through the six years the kids were in college and the two years after that when we were paying the deferred loans, we managed not to touch our retirement savings.

All of these financial manipulations are nice, but what is behind them is plenty of hard work. Besides all of the goal setting and financial planning, both Pat and I were working. I was basically working two jobs: my main full time job and my part time job with the National Guard. My wife was working full-time and taking up the family slack of me working 15 days straight every month. This created a good income stream, but also meant that we worked a lot, but we also had to put in the effort to create family time for each other and the children. Wednesday morning breakfast at the 99 cent special breakfast place after dropping our kids at high school became a really big deal for our survival as a couple.

I have tried to end this chapter several times, but have always thought of something else to tell you. All of this focus on money for yourself may seem a bit selfish and it is, but it is the only way to insure that you are taking care of the life you will have after the kids are on their own. If you are like most parents, you want to give everything to your children and you will, including your own retirement savings, if you don't have the discipline to think about your wife and yourself and that little corner of the world you will share later, together.

I am not so selfish that I have forgotten my children and grandchildren. We do help them as we see a need. It is just that the lion's share of our good fortune, at least in their eyes, will come later as you will read in the coming sections.

Chapter 10: Investment vs. Speculation
I want it all. I want it now!

As I've said before, time is really on your side when you are young and less so as you get older. This is true with finances and your life skills as well.

When you are young, you make mistakes. We all do and we have a lifetime to make up for them. Our fellow inhabitants of the planet are young, too, and also making blunders as they learn, so they are very forgiving of our inadequacies. As we get older, we hopefully learn from the mistakes that we have made and get wiser in our decision making and require forgiveness less often. That's not really about money or investing, but just living your life in general. But patience is something you learn as a life lesson and this can be a very useful quality as an investment tool. The younger you learn the value of patience, the more dividends (no pun intended) it will pay.

A case in point is the desire to own a vacation home or the dream of a time-share. We see that vacation home as an idyllic existence void of any of the mundane daily routines...a living in paradise at the beach with someone continuously replenishing our margarita glass and refreshing the salt on the endless rim. In reality, if we live there we have to pay the mortgage, do the grocery shopping, and make our own margaritas. And don't get me started on the maintenance fees for that time-share! The lesson here is to be patient, research, and learn before you leap.

Time-share presentations had become a joke for us in the 1980's because they were such a bad deal and they still are today...we knew we would never be tempted to buy, but they kept inviting us. Not just that, but they were willing to give us free gifts just for going. TV's, free weekends, money...all for attending a 90-minute presentation. We would often make bets about the final price of the time-share and see what the cost was after the "manager" came over to offer the: "final, once-in-a-lifetime, never-to-be-duplicated, good today only, just-for-you deal." It was all great fun and enjoyable for awhile. That is until they started offering free airline tickets that had so many blackout dates that you could never use them. So, we stopped going and eventually the promotion companies stopped asking.

I once called a salesman's bluff at one of these presentations. I asked him how much it had cost to build the whole complex. I then did some quick math to show that they were selling individual condos for $1,000,000 each (if you counted all 52 time-share weeks)...which paid for the whole complex after 20 or so units and then after selling them for this ridiculously inflated price, they had the gall to charge rent in the form of "maintenance" of $50,000 per unit every year. (That's $1,000 per week for each individual owner...forever...you could rent similar units for the maintenance fee alone never mind "buying" into the resort.) The salesman got very quiet and we left with our "prizes." There was no manager's special price that day.

Anyway, a time-share is worse than owning a boat and I think a boat would be a lot more fun. Someone I know tried to get rid of a time-share. Not an easy thing to do. It's worse than trying to cure herpes. In fact there are companies that will take the time-share off your hands, if you pay them a fee, because the maintenance fees are a binding forever contract even to your heirs. Some people pay to get out of the contract just to get rid of the perpetual maintenance fee.

Day trading or trying to beat the stock market is best left to the professionals. They can afford to lose money because they are not playing with their own. For the individual investor, it is best to buy stocks of companies that make a real product and thereby make money. Real products are always in demand, especially if they are good stuff. If you use it, it probably is good and your friends use it, too. Invest in things you know about and accounts that have a guaranteed return. Companies that pay dividends help you save more through lean times and earn you more shares.

I like the ponies. That is I enjoy going to the race track and bet on the horses. I've made money a few times, but mostly I've lost and I still go back because I love the atmosphere. My favorite track is in Saratoga, New York. It is one of the oldest tracks in the country and they only race there in August. The smell of the fresh cut grass and the finely combed earth are sights and smells that excite me. During the meet at Saratoga, bands play all day, there is a huge family picnic area behind the grandstand under some old growth trees and they parade the horses through the crowd on their way to the paddock. If you are a fan, you can't get any closer to the action. My wife and I really enjoy the day and we camp close by in our motor home...we always love a trip to upstate New York. It is all about enjoyment and memories and mostly we don't earn any money, but we have a fun time.

I don't treat my investments like a day at the races. I don't bet on long shots and I don't take chances. I want sure performance (profits) and a stable run. In horse racing only the first four finishers make money...the fourth barely enough to cover the entry fee. With stocks, they can all make money and I expect them to from the start or I would not buy them. I'm not looking for the "thrill of victory" with my investments. If you seek outlandish returns you often find the "agony of defeat."

I like stocks that pay quarterly dividends. They are not flashy and they do not always make the headlines on the financial pages, but they provide steady growth in their value, grow themselves by reinvesting dividends, and in the end give you something back. I have made a couple of blunders through the years, but mostly we have done well.

Pat and I have a portfolio of about a dozen diversified stocks and funds. There are both large cap and small cap companies. They all pay dividends and I invested in them all the same way...except for one. The one is a large company that I already told you about. I got that from a company plan when I left the company and have never sold it. It has been a real winner in the growth and dividend department.

As for the others...I did some research and initially bought between $3,000 and $10,000 worth of stock in each company over time. I also signed up to invest $100 per month automatically from my checking account in each stock. I don't forget about them and hope for the best...I have an on-line portfolio tracker that is free and I check it regularly so I can smile. Along with my other accounts, things have worked out nicely.

The $100 per month investment (I started with$50 because that was all I could afford.) is the most important part of my message to you. I did not do this all at once. I started with one and as my income grew I increased the number of my investments. All of this is completely independent of any former workplace so that it is mine and completely portable…no matter where or if I was working there.

So, I have never received a "company match." If you have this opportunity, take it…snatch it…grab it…tackle it…hold on and don't let go. It is the best investment you can have. You put in money and the company either matches or partially matches it. The money that the company puts in is a benefit from the company. This instantly multiplies your money and pays ever increasing dividends over time. This can build you a giant portfolio over the years. If you have this opportunity, run to your HR office and sign up, today!

I'm always in it for the long haul. When I invest, I am a company owner. I watch new products and expect the company to keep growing. If they didn't, I wouldn't have bought them in the first place. Some have taken a while to come around, but they have continually grown because they increased in value, reinvested the dividends, and I continued to invest $100 per month. There have been only two years in which I have lost money with my portfolio…everyone else lost in those years…probably a lot more than I did.

Anyway…my stance is buy and hold. I like solid investments and I don't really take big chances. This may not be glamorous, but I sleep at night and in the long run I have grown my portfolio to a level that the dividend payouts alone more than sustains my retirement living. Remember that when you buy and sell stocks through a broker, you pay a brokerage fee…that is how they make money. And make it they do. It doesn't matter if you do. The fees apply to every move you make. No wonder they encourage you to buy and sell.

Tracking your investments is important. It means you are paying attention and pay attention you should. It's up to you. Pay someone else to pay attention and give them part of your profit or pay attention yourself. How else would you know how close you are to reaching your goal and knowing when you have reached that magic number?

Chapter 11: Others Have Good Ideas, Too
Listen!

That's right. You don't have to know it all. I certainly don't and most certainly knew even less back when I started. So, how could I have the confidence to handle my own finances and build the wealth that I have? I read what other smart people write. I don't always take their advice because many times their words are tainted by who they work for or who they are trying to influence or I just don't like or understand the idea. So, I make up my own mind as to what makes sense and act accordingly, but many times it is based on what other people say and think. I only take part in investments that make sense to me and those that I can understand.

If you have a broker, you pay about 1% or more of your portfolio for this advice that is really available free in the financial pages of newspapers and magazines. This 1% loss over time can be the difference between reaching your goal(s) and falling short. These days with exchange traded funds (ETF's) and funds sold by discount brokers, you can keep your expenses down to 0.2 % or less and have the benefit of someone handling your portfolio. If you lack the confidence to make a go of it on your own, this is a viable solution.

When something sounds too good to be true, it most certainly is...and nothing is as bad as it seems. There are financial writers that love to see the market go up and down. It not only gives them something to write about, but they can influence the market in ways they would like to see it go. Many of these market influencers go to jail for using inside information, most don't. But just realize that it is not your meager retirement savings driving the markets or interest rates. You are at best along for the ride, but there are a lot of you so realize there are trends involved.

Those trends and the resulting movement of money rule the financial world. You need to pay attention to this information. If this is hard for you to follow, maybe you do need professional advice and this is nothing to be concerned with nor do I look down on those that use financial professionals as somehow lacking in ability...maybe they just don't have the time or the inclination to keep track of it all.

So, you can get a financial advisor and maybe you should, but beware. Many try to sell you their own products because they make commissions on what they sell...that is above the fee they are charging you for the advice and the piece of your profit pie that they take. I just didn't have the stomach for giving my savings away. It's hard enough to come by and keep as it is. If you need these services, get them and get your savings going. It is better to give away a portion of your earnings to an advisor than to have no earnings at all.

But I'm not above taking some free advice. I've sent for free publications from brokers. Advertised titles like *'Are you on the right track to retirement?'* Why not? They want to give it away as a promotion, I'll take it. I take their step by step advice and compare it to what I have done and my future plans. I have taken many of these types of suggestions and put them to work for me. Online there is the *DRIP Investor* which provides a list of dividend reinvestment plans, my favorite way to invest. They write a newsletter and send it directly to my inbox. I also subscribe to *"The Motley Fool"* another investor advice newsletter.

I treasure my subscription to *"Money"* magazine and *"Bottom Line Personal."* These are two publications I would recommend. They tend to write about people looking to build a nest egg and offer advice...often step-by-step plans to individual investing. You can take some of these plans and customize them for yourself and implement all or part of the plan as your own. "Money" has ceased publication and their subscribers have switched to *"Kiplingers"* which I find very similar and equally informing. Even the Sunday paper and its Money section offer interesting reading on investments and saving money. The *USA Today* has a money section it publishes every day with topics of interest for the young investor and retirees alike. But don't hang your hat on every-day market quotes. It will drive you batty and cost you sleep. It is best to stick with your long-term plan and don't be swayed by the day to day market activity.

In short, if you do not want to pay for advice, you need to seek it out. There is no way you can figure it all out in your head. There are some smart people out there...many of them would like to have some of your money...the challenge is to keep most of it for yourself.

Chapter 12: The Big Mistake

There we were. Like two kids with our noses pressed against the plate glass window of *FAO Swartz* in New York City drooling over the new toy that lay just beyond our reach displayed within. Could we have it; please, pretty please? It was the object of our dreams that we had desired for years. But it had a catch...of course.

We were sitting on the sofa in our living room watching one of those shows where a couple is looking for their dream vacation house at the beach, on a lake, or up in the mountains. You know the one's I mean. The couple is lead by a local realtor on a quest for their perfect mountain/beach/woods retreat. Then they meet up at a local pub to talk over what they have seen and decide on their dream vacation home; instant nirvana!

I picked up my smart phone from the side table and made a simple inquiry: *lake houses in Rhode Island*. A state map popped up with dots indicating the many "dream" homes for sale located on a lake in our small state. I had limited my search because there was always a problem for us with owning a vacation home; the distance to get there. Maine has the pristine atmosphere we love with forest and beach, but most of the vacation properties in our price range are four to five hours away. The commute for a weekend was just too far. That would limit our use of the property and make it not worth the investment.

Looking at the map, I zeroed in on a few lake properties in the northern portion of the state within a forty-five minute drive of our present home. As I expanded the map, the price displayed next to the location dot. Wow! If you want a lake house having a significant amount of cash-on-hand seemed to be a prerequisite to buying one. As I studied further, one property in our price range emerged. I tepidly touched the dot to get more information.

What emerged was an inquiry into a property on a lake in northwestern Rhode Island. The description, price, and location seemed about right for us and the one picture provided was promising. I began swiping the picture to examine more about the property. What they showed was a lake house cottage with three bedrooms, an open kitchen/sitting room, and a huge screened-in porch overlooking the lake. There were two sheds and a dock included. The lake itself looked beautiful. I was more than intrigued.

Pat of course continued to watch her program. When it came to a commercial I said, "If you think what you're watching is nice, take a look at this." I handed her my phone. She scrolled through the pictures and asked me where the house was. Not too much else was said, but we both continued to look at the pictures of the lake house. I looked several times throughout the day. I'm sure she did, too.

I'm not certain who suggested it first, but we decided to take a ride and look at the property. After all, it was a beautiful day for a ride in the convertible and no one charges for just looking; right?

It was a great ride along the rural routes of northern Rhode Island with the top down on the Mustang and what is left of my hair blowing in the breeze. It took some doing, but we found the gravel entry road. The sign said "Residents only" but we soldiered on. How else were we supposed to see the property?

Our GPS directed us to take the right fork in the road and like Yogi said, we took it. There were many cars parked at several cottages. It was a Sunday and many lake residences had visitors. The lake itself was a bustle of boat traffic with skiers and jet boats creating wakes that both used for their enjoyment.

The cottage looked good from close up, but no one was in residence so an outside look was all we got. We found a turn around and left the area. We stopped at a local spot for lunch on the way back and continued to talk about the possibilities of owning a lake house.

The next day we hit the *inquire* button on the web site and we were contacted by a real estate agent. A couple of phone calls later; we had an appointment to tour the cottage later in the week.

We all met at the appointed time; our real estate agent, the agent for the owner, along with Pat and me. The property was perfect for us. Three bedrooms, the large living and kitchen area, huge screened in porch, water rights, and a dock. There was one problem. The property had not been used in some time and had fallen into some disrepair. Nothing was falling down mind you, but outside stairways were showing signs of decay, the pier at the dock needed repair, and the inside...well, we're not hard to please, but it needed some TLC.

There were a couple of other items that caused us concern. First, the cottage was on leased land. That meant we didn't own the property that the house sat on although we would own the house. Second, because it was on leased land, the bank would not allow a mortgage and the deal had to be cash.

The first concern was alleviated by the owner's agent who happened to be a long time resident of the compound and also paid rent to the same land owner. The residents had an association that had an agreement with the landowner that in the event of a sale, the present residents would have the right-of-first-refusal on purchasing the property. That meant that the land could not be sold out from under us, so to speak, for development or any other purpose.

The second concern became more problematical during our negotiation for the purchase of the cottage. Most negotiations for real estate purchases are quite formal. Legal bid forms are completed and submitted by the buyers. The sellers then accept, reject, or counter offer. This lengthy process goes back a forth a few times until an agreement is reached; or not and the process is terminated.

In a cash sale, the process is much more direct. We called our agent with an offer. While on the phone with us, our agent called the seller's agent on another line. He made a counter offer, which she told us. I countered that…he countered and said the sellers would accept if we could close in thirty days. We said yes.

Thus began the quest to liquidate some assets to meet the cash payment. First, I found out that selling investment assets and having cash in your hand doesn't work quite that quickly. Then, I thought of liquidating our 403b plan. That had enough money in it, but I couldn't turn that around quickly enough to meet the thirty day closing demand.

I went to our bank and met with one of the managers and told him what I was up against. We discussed it for awhile. He verified that I could not get a mortgage against the property because of the leased land, discussed other types of loans, and we finally hit on a solution. I could take a personal loan using my CD's as collateral. Remember the ladder CD's I spoke of earlier? Those are the ones I would use until the money would come in from the 403b plan which I could then use to pay off the loan and we would again be debt-free and own the lake house outright.

Why would we do such a thing as buy a lake house at this late stage of the game? Pat and I had been lamenting the demise of our weekly Tuesday dinners with the grandchildren. This practice began when our oldest daughter moved to her own apartment. She would come weekly to do her laundry at our house and we would all have dinner. Fast forward many years...our two daughters with their children would come to our house every Tuesday night for dinner...laundry not included. This went on for some time until it just...stopped.

Grandchildren create their own schedule driven by school, sports, and other activities that then dominate their parents' lives. This in-turn led to no night in the week that everyone was available and the Tuesday night dinners became a thing of the past. But if we had a lake house, maybe we could reclaim some of our time together and create memories with our children and our grandchildren. That's why we bought the lake house.

The financing went through as I described and we closed on the lake house within thirty days. All was well until the finances were complete and the loan was paid off. A 403b account is an IRA. Money is deducted from your paycheck before taxes. This reduces your tax burden while you are still working. Remember I had established this account to pay for healthcare for Pat and I between the ages of 60 and 65 when Medicare would kick in. I didn't have to use it because of the Tricare benefit I received from the National Guard. So, that money had been sitting there, still growing, and I really had no plans for it...that is until the lake house purchase.

The amount in the 403b account was about the purchase price of the lake house. Easy...cash it in and it becomes a lake house...free money...not so fast! Because the money was deducted pretax from my pay check, the taxes must now be paid. What most people do is establish an annuity with the money and pay the taxes a little at a time. I had withdrawn all of the money at once so the taxman wanted his money and he wanted it now!

The company that managed the 403b removed 20% from the total and sent it to the government before I even got the check. Then, I had to report the total as income on my tax return causing an avalanche of problems in the higher bracket. This also left me short on paying off the loan and I had to use some of my savings to pay off the short term loan at the bank.

Okay...Okay...I knew some of that was going to happen, but in my euphoria I didn't think it would be that bad. No...that wasn't the end of it. At the end of the following year, Pat and I received a letter from Medicare. Because we had exceeded income limits for the previous year, our Medicare payments would now be $190 per month instead of $134. At least that is only for a year and the payments will return to normal the following year because my reported income will return to normal.

So I call it *The Big Mistake*. Financially, paying for the lake house turned out to be more like I carried a mortgage rather than a cash purchase. I paid all of that interest I would have paid the bank with a mortgage to Uncle Sam. Maybe I'll get a thank you card. What I should have done was to carry the debt for a few years and draw down the 403b $20,000 at a time. That would have spread the taxes out over time, but I hate debt and was anxious to be rid of it.

On the other hand we have started to enjoy time at the lake with our family and grandchildren. Possibly, I should have bought the lake house years ago. Our hope is that we can continue to build memories on the lake and that our children's families will enjoy the lake house long after we are gone. That will make it all worth it.

Chapter 13: Should I Get a Financial Advisor?

If you are following the sequence so far, there are many things that a person can do to save money for retirement. Finding employment that offers a matching IRA, a stock savings plan, or retirement plan is a great starting point. On your own, investing in stocks and/or bonds help your savings grow independently of your job. Ladder CD's and money market accounts can fill in gaps of your savings plan and provide an emergency fund. Managing all of this takes focus and determination along with a lot of planning and research.

All of that energy is why I encourage people to put things on automatic. Make decisions annually and formulate a plan, put the decisions into action, and then follow through. That's all great, but how do you keep track of it all. Two ways; first, you are young and your mind can keep track of many things at once; second, once a decision is made; put it on automatic. That is, if you decide to save $100 per month in any way shape or form, make arrangements with your financial institution to withdraw the money from your account and put it where you want to save it. As an alternative, you can have the place you want to save your cash withdraw it from your checking account every month. The holding company will also send you monthly or quarterly statements as to the progress of your savings.

Automatic savings is the key; set it and forget it. I don't care if you save $10, $20, $100, or $1000 per month...it happens every month, adds to your savings along with your interest eventually creating a nest egg for your retirement. Should you put it all in one place? Never!

Banks have FDIC limits to protect your savings, but there are dollar limits to those protections per account and per institution. You should know what those are. Also, if you invest in stocks, there are few protections other than to diversify. Markets fluctuate and so do the values of your investments. Some investments are "safer" than others. You should know about those as well.

If you start this entire savings strategy back in your thirties, you will make several changes, additions, and manipulations as you adjust your savings plan with life alterations such as raises, the birth of children, and hopefully a rising salary. Your forties and your fifties bring the financial life altering events such as college for those children, weddings, and grandchildren. Things sure do become clearer and more stable as you approach your retirement date, but from your twenties and thirties it looks like your goals might never come into focus; especially from that distance.

But let's consider that you have made it. You have comfortably retired with enough income to keep you enjoying the lifestyle to which you have become accustomed, as they say. What now? I found that for the first couple of years, there was still considerable manipulation to be done. Not the least of which was shifting from a savings mentality to a spending mentality. In fact for the first few years, I continued on the savings plan because I could afford it and my savings were continually growing.

But after a time, inflation was taking hold and I needed to withdraw some money from my savings to keep up. This meant shifting from continual reinvestment, to withdrawing some of my market gain to sustain our lifestyle. It also meant reversing the "set it and forget it" mentality plans that I had set up over the years.

As an example, one of my five "ladder CD's" comes up for renewal every December. Remember, I had set up five CD accounts of CD's each with a five-year maturity date. Each year I received a letter from the bank and had to appear to renew my CD for another five years. The decisions I could make were: leave the profits to grow, take the profit, and/or the terms of renewal. Early on in retirement, I left the profits to grow, but as time wore on I took the profit and left only the principal upon renewal of the CD. This had been the extent of my involvement in manipulating my investments once it was on automatic.

Now it is time to do it for all of my accounts. CD's, stocks, bonds, IRA's...the works. To unravel all of those investments and shift from automatic savings to a "send me the profits" mode was daunting and I realized I wasn't as mentally young as I used to be. I needed some advice and I needed to assemble my investments in one place so that I could withdraw what I needed in future years. I needed a place that with just one phone call, I could have access to my finances. I needed a financial advisor.

Through my dealings with my church, I had met a gentleman from a large financial services firm. He acted as financial advisor for our church and seemed very level headed. His fees for the services provided were also very low which you know is important to me. We met over coffee to see if my needs could be served by his company.

Even with his help, I would have to transfer my holdings one at a time to the new firm. This would require some involvement on my part, but in the end it would be worth it. I would have all of my holdings in one place which would put all of my equities on one annual statement. This would make it easier for me to file my taxes. Also, the firm would hold my dividend payments, pay interest on that cash account, and send me an amount of my choosing every month.

It took a couple of months to get it all done, but in the end it was worth it. The access to financial tools provided on the website was worth the price of admission. Some of the companies holding my assets made it difficult for me to transfer the funds because they didn't want to lose a customer. Little by little the job got done and now I get payments directly into my bank account with regularity; more about this later.

I make contact with my financial advisor a couple of times each year. I still make my own financial goals, but I discuss them with him and he provides guidance. This offers some peace of mind to this aging financial brain leaving me time to think about other important things like fishing and vacation planning.

As the financial markets get more complex, I realize that I need this professional advice. Over the last twenty years, it really has been easy for a non-professional like me to make money in the stock market. The buy and hold philosophy with reputable companies was a sure winner. Oh, I made a couple of flubs that cost me ten or twenty thousand dollars, but most of my investments paid off well in a burgeoning economy. Stock splits, dividend reinvestment, and monthly contributions to my accounts over twenty years made for a winning formula. Now it was time to spend someone else's money.

Chapter 14: Spending Someone Else's Money

The whole idea of saving for retirement is that you can have money to live after you stop working. Makes sense doesn't it. I thought so, too. That had been my goal since I was forty and started down this road to financial success. I diligently squirreled away my hard earned cash, gladly went without at times, all in the hopes that one day I could tap that cash to support myself after I quit working for a living. I was wrong. Not so much was I wrong about saving for retirement, but I was looking at it incorrectly.

No...No... The advice that I have given you about financial independence in retirement is true. I just was a bit off in stating my goals. You see, I was thinking about having this giant pot of cash and as the financial gurus will tell you; withdrawing 4% per year to live on. As the joke goes, you hope that if you plan it right, you use up all of your money before you die and if you plan it perfectly; your last check bounces.

Well, I have found that in the wisdom of my years; that's not exactly right. What is right is, if you do it correctly; you basically have enough investments to live off someone else's money. How's that, you ask? It's about the dividends and interest. Think of it this way. If you had enough money and put it in the bank, you could live off the interest and never touch the principal. That preserves your wealth for future generations and gives you money to live and enjoy your retirement.

That's a really big bank account, you say; and you'd be right. You certainly need investments that pay more than simple interest at the bank. I didn't realize it at the time I was doing it, that's why I say I was wrong, but tapping into the financial system that pays more than simple interest is what I had been doing all along. It is the secret of the rich and famous, so to speak. Certainly it is the secret of families that have become wealthy. It is what insurance companies do when they sell you an annuity. It is what states do when they pay out lottery winnings over time. Both the insurance companies and the states give the annuity owner the interest and keep the principal for themselves.

Most of us grind away at the office, on the road, or on the telephone day after day making a living. That takes pretty much all of our energy and creativity leaving time for little else than a two-week cruise around the Caribbean to nowhere. Then we come back to work and do it again. What a life!

That rat race gives us an existence, but that's not a life. There has to be more. The more is time; time to be creative. We watch shows like "Shark Tank" where someone comes up with one unique idea that sets off a chain reaction to true wealth. What is true wealth? Is it a pile of money? No. It is the time to do what you want...free time. And that leads to more time that your brain is free to think of more ideas that lead to more creative things that leads to more wealth. Get the idea? It's all about free time.

The obstacle to that kind of success is the time and commitment to make it happen. Most of those people have sold their soul to get their product (idea) to where it is. They put everything else aside, or they were that desperate, to put their heart and soul into one thing. Most of us don't have that kind of commitment or are not willing to take that kind of a risk.

Let's leave the philosophical discussion and get back to the realities of your retirement plan and living off someone else's money and your retirement nest egg. It is great to talk about providing for your future family and we'll soon get to that, but your retirement comes first. Here's what I now think. Planning to live off someone else's money or letting your money work for you is my new way of thinking about providing money to fund your retirement.

Let's put all the steps we have been talking about together and take a look at the end game. You have got yourself a job with a matching IRA plan or a defined benefit retirement plan. What is that? A certain portion of your paycheck is given over to a financial firm that invests the money...your money. After a given time on the job, they promise to pay you a certain amount of money per month for as long as you live. If you live a reasonable time, you will certainly collect more than you put into the account. That is living off someone else's money.

If you serve over twenty years in the military, either full-time or the National Guard, the government will pay you a pension along with other benefits. You did not contribute anything other than your time for this. I will say that you have risked your life and limb for this benefit, but that might be another book. The money they send to you every month is living off someone else's money.

Remember those ladder CD's? They yield about $1500 to $2000 per year depending on the prevailing interest rate.

You have given over about $18,000 of your money to the bank and they pay you interest. You then take the interest after five years and then reinvest the original $18,000 back into another five year CD. You end up with a profit every year that adds to your income. That is living off someone else's money.

The stocks I hold pay dividends every quarter. That dividend is deposited into my account at the financial firm. It accrues throughout the year and also pays interest. I withdraw $1,000 per month or $12,000 per year. That is added to the pensions that my wife and I collect from our jobs, along with my federal pension from serving in the National Guard, which is added to the profit from my ladder CD every year, my small income from social security, and my dividend check every month from my stock holdings. That is my total income that provides more than I need to live, keep up my house, update my cars and RV, and pays my bills with fun-money left over every month. That's living off someone else's money while still growing the principal as a legacy fund for my family.

So, our retirement is funded by my wife and me investing ourselves, our working lives, to fund our retirement. Now let's talk about the legacy. Why is that so important to me? There are many reasons. Providing opportunity for my grandchildren is definitely important. It also provides peace of mind for my children. If all works out well, it will also provide opportunity for future generations. Remember I talked about time to be creative; the time to come up with that one fabulous idea or nurture that one great talent. My legacy is that I provide that to my progeny which will last and last long after I am gone.

I had stated that I was concerned about future generations and their saving for retirement. I can't solve everyone's problems, but I can give my own children and my grandchildren a boost. This legacy fund is that boost.

Chapter 15: Priorities

Who's on first?

As was stated earlier, life is about choices. Sometimes benevolence is a good thing and helping others is the right thing to do. But sometimes, you need to be a little selfish. You should never sacrifice the future for something you want right now. When you spend money, such as borrowing from your IRA primarily meant to finance your retirement, you are stealing from your future to finance immediate satisfaction. This is the biggest mistake you can make when it comes to retirement saving. It is almost like not saving at all.

And the same goes for your children. There is a point in family life where we all struggle; such as, when your wife is home raising the kids and not working because you have both decided that it is the right thing to do. During that time, you are working as much overtime as you can get and still robbing Peter to pay Paul when it comes to paying the bills. You put your nose to the grindstone for your family, but at some time there needs to be a shift where helping should never leave you in the lurch for the future.

Remember I talked about the time my kids were both in college and our bank account went down to less than $900. This situation had happened before when we were in our 20's, but saving for retirement didn't matter as much then. The drop in our savings account while the kids were in college was calculated and we were still in our early forties and had time to catch up on our retirement savings. We were not saving as much then and we didn't have a lot in long-term savings, but what we had was untouchable. That long-term saving represented the future and to my way of thinking, the future was only 18 years away...when we turned 60 years old. As soon as the kids were out of school, it was full speed ahead on the savings. That money we were spending for college became that money we were saving for ourselves. We did not take the reward for getting through the college years right away in the form of new cars for ourselves and such; rather we are enjoying it now a few years later.

Kids struggle and you always want to help. My wife always told me to leave enough in the checking account so there is money there when she wants it. Part of that includes helping our children in their young adult lives. But never, and she understands this well, did I make money from our retirement savings or our emergency account available. It was too great a risk and we would probably never recover. Yes, I am a disciplined SOB. I set goals and make plans and generally stick with them. I adjust and reorganize my financial plans once per year and then spend the year executing that plan. That's why I didn't have to pay a financial planner back then. If you don't have this kind of discipline, perhaps you do need a planner to accomplish your retirement savings goal.

You have to look at saving money as a mathematical multiplication problem. A dollar that you save today, will multiply many times over...that is only true for so long...the so long is the number of years you have to save. It is very true when you are in your twenties. It is still true when you are in your thirties. But the margin grows smaller as you pass through your forties and during your fifties; the multiplication begins to become like addition because the older you get; time and the magic of compound interest is no longer on your side.

When you reach retirement, as my wife would say, it is what it is. Not that you're done building your wealth, but now it is different. You are building for the future of your children and grandchildren while securing your own. At this stage, your helping focus turns more toward your grandchildren. Your future is now secure, and your money is working to keep you secure and to build a future for your children and beyond...as I spoke from my soap box as I was articulating my dream for their future. I wonder if anyone was listening.

So, here it was five years later and now almost ten years and what is happening with my saving now? I'm doing the same as I did before. What! You say. I thought it was now time to spend...spend...spend. It is, but it turns out that we don't spend as much as I thought. The retirement checks are more than enough to keep us in the "lifestyle we have become accustomed." No we're not pinching pennies anymore, but we have a nice house...paid for...two nice cars...paid for...and a nice motor home...paid for. Without any excess bills hanging over our heads, the retirement checks and the "gap" money provided by the dividend checks from our stock holdings are enough to keep us happy.

I'll tell you what the savings do for us though. It came to be that we needed a new(er) motor home. We of course traded in our old one and paid cash out of our reserve for the newer one. No loan...no interest...no payment because our stock portfolio is still growing. I have ceased the automatic investing every month and now a portion of the dividends from the stocks come to us in the form of income every month. So, as I have said...we are living on other people's money. That is the kind of money, i.e. profit that now pays for the extras in our life like a newer motor home.

The purpose to saving now has different thinking attached to it. Along with providing financial security for us, we are now thinking about the financial security of our children and that of our grandchildren. Both of our children are financially sound, but the future is always uncertain. At some point we would like to help to secure that future. Also, our grandchildren are growing up. We try to help with their needs and are considering what we can do to help with their education and help to secure their future as well.

There is a legacy to be considered here. If we are successful in leaving a financial legacy behind, that would mean even more success for our children and our grandchildren. That will be something we can really be proud of because that will leave our family in great financial shape for generations to come.

The message here is to always keep your savings priorities straight. Don't sacrifice your future for satisfaction today. If you are greatly tempted to spend $10, spend five to be satisfied and save the other five. Nothing works for savings better than making it automatic.

When I worked for the government, I also had a part-time job one night per week that was attached to the same agency. At first, it only paid about $25 per session. We got a separate check for this and getting a check for less than $20 after taxes wasn't much and generally the checks were cashed and spent without much notice. Instead of having these checks come to my home in the mail, I elected to have them sent to my credit union account at work. Checks for $20 were cashed and easily squandered. Besides, they were an annoyance and I would have had to go to the bank every week. I stayed at this job for ten years so you can imagine my very pleasant surprise when I checked my balance in that account after a few years.

There was no on-line banking then and we did not receive regular statements from the company credit union, but you could stop by the office at any time to check your balance or make withdrawals. But the office was in another building and it was not until I was promoted that I had the opportunity to visit that other building more often and discover the magic of automatic savings. Those checks went up with my military promotion and I was now making twice what I was per session and the savings were rising at more than twice the rate with interest which was considerably higher back then.

Today, with on-line banking, your savings progress is easily tracked. Also, there is the opportunity of direct deposit for your paycheck. You can even have portions of your direct deposit sent to different accounts or easily transfer money using your on-line account. Automatic bill pay from designated accounts is also easily arranged. All of these services make it easy to keep up your accounts and bills for travel. Before retirement, these services were helpful in transferring money to gain the greatest interest as our savings grew.

Your family and your future should always be your financial priorities. Take care of them both because both are irreplaceable and will always be there for you.

Chapter 16: Enough Is Enough

When do you know?

There is this wonderful feeling you get when you check the balance on your checking account and there is an adequate amount of money in there to make you feel comfortable. There is a serious question in that for you. What is enough cash to make you feel comfortable? We all feel pretty comfortable when the paycheck hits the account at the beginning of the month, but what about on the 25th or the 26th? How comfortable are you feeling then?

During your working life, if you got paid every two weeks, "enough" was enough money to pay the bills. That is, you got paid, sat down at your desk and wrote out checks for the monthly bills, and there was still a positive balance in the checkbook. Even better, there was enough of a balance left in that checkbook to pay other bills that may come in for the next two weeks and enough cash to put a jingle in your pocket. Ah, that was great. And as your work life progressed, you put some money into savings, some into investments, some into the rainy day fund, and still had some left over. If you got to this point, you were living the high life! The key to being financially secure is not living beyond your means.

Fear! That is the key to advertising and selling. Invoke a fear in people and they will run out to buy your product. Show them how poor their life is without it...they just have to have it...you're a fool if you don't buy this. Create a market by creating a need that may never have existed before and sell, sell, sell. I didn't know that my dry eyes were chronic...I must have to do something...sure I do...buy this stuff and use it every day...you're hooked for life. The point is not to just "sell" you something, but get you on a monthly fee schedule. Then, you become an income stream...they won't call you that, but rather you are a valued customer and your call is important to us...that check you send is definitely more important and if you want to hear that pitch in English...please press 1.

So, how about we look at this situation differently? We look at accumulating enough wealth to retire comfortably as a very real possibility. Something you can do without wearing clothes rescued from the rag heap and driving a fifteen year old Plymouth. If you have tastes that run to the very newest and the very latest, it will be a problem for you to ever be satisfied. If you have the mindset that this is good and works for me and it doesn't create so much angst when you buy it that you lie awake at night wondering why you did it...you may be very well on the way to understanding what "enough" for you really is.

We in our American society have been told that we need more, more, more. It is a condition that permeates our mind reinforced by advertising and TV talk shows. Travel around this country and look at how most people live. They have their families, a job, and a place to live. Granted some are "better" off than others on all counts, but it depends on who the judge is, doesn't it? If a person was unemployed and now has a minimum wage job, he thinks that is great. If a person had that minimum wage job and gets a skilled job that pays more, he thinks that is great. If a person has a good job and gets a promotion, he is elated. Get the point? Things can always get better, but when do you know you are happy and secure?

There are people in this world that most would consider poor, yet they are happy. Their house doesn't look that great, but they have one. Grandma and Grandpa live with Mom and Dad with the four kids, yet we see them gathered around the dinner table elated to be together. We see contented people all the time and wonder how it is that they are satisfied. When do you know? When do you stop striving and start enjoying?

The term "enough" cannot have a universal definition. It is the point at which you sigh with contentment and feel that you have achieved what you were looking for and look at life as though it is your oyster. Wouldn't we all like to get there? But as the song says, "It's a long road out of Eden." The lyrics of this Eagles tune try to show us that we all want too much and are driven to excess. We all want to own and dominate and that there is never enough. But there is and it can be for you.

Get your head out of the clouds and don't want so much. Dare I say; set your sights lower? Not lower on the achievement scale, but lesser on the accumulation scale. It is not the one with the most toys that wins, but rather the one with the toys that mean the most and many of these don't cost money. Friendship, camaraderie, relationships, and heart make your life happy. It is great to have a boat. But instead if you have a friend with a boat that you can go fishing with...it's even better.

It's not about having the boat, but having the friend and going fishing. The boat could be yours; it doesn't matter. The point is to share it with someone and that makes it better. Sitting in the boat fishing alone all the time, no matter the luxuriousness of the boat is a lonely experience, even if you can afford it. Surrounded by wonderful things will be meaningless if all you leave behind when you go are the things. It will mean that you have accumulated much, but had nothing at all.

There is a group of friends from the National Guard that I meet with regularly. When I see these people, it is like no time has passed by. I have been out of the Guard for over twenty-five years, but it doesn't matter. Our shared memories will keep us close forever. We have slept, eaten, and worked together to a point that we know each other well...well enough to last a lifetime. Some people will never know this kind of closeness with others and for that I feel sad and that we lose something as a nation. But those are thoughts for writing another time.

The point is to find enough of this in your life, supported by sufficient finances to enjoy it, which will define this sort of contentment for you. We have talked about how you accumulate enough wealth to support your retirement goals, but finances are only half the story. The other half is to accumulate enough emotional capital to support you in your life to create happiness and that will generate contentment and at that point you will know you have *enough*.

Chapter 17: Spur of the Moment Decisions
= Stupid

Before we go any further, I feel the need to talk about overall decision making. We all make hundreds of decisions every day and most of them do not require much thought. The light is green; so I go. I put my left shoe on and then my right. I think I'll get some water. These are all decisions of little consequence and require little forethought. I'm talking here about decisions that matter.

Should I invest more money in stocks? Should I put this money in a CD? Should I open an IRA? Should I increase my contribution to my retirement plan at work? What health care plan should I choose? These financial decisions and many other decisions concerning your family and your life matter very much and should not be taken lightly.

Decisions that have long-term effects should be given the consideration and thought they deserve. The seriousness and impact of the decision should be proportional to the time it takes to make it. With all the information out there, research about important matters takes time. The misinformation given by sales reps and brokers is all about making the sale, not about helping you. For instance, I would not make a decision about health care plans right after listening to a company's presentation. But don't fall into the black hole of decision-making. That black hole is that you're thinking about it and you never make a decision at all. That's as bad as making a snap judgment and paying dearly for it later.

Sometimes not deciding right away gives perspective to your thinking and clarity about which decision to make.

Sleeping on it is a real decision making philosophy. I once heard a story about decision making that on its face seems almost comical, but has profound meaning to giving matters careful consideration.

Say a railroad car full of lettuce comes in and the inspector is not quite sure that it is of the quality of the company standard. He orders that the car be put on a side track until he can examine it further. He leaves it there for a time while he attends to other matters. When he's ready, he examines the lettuce and finds that it is wilted and brown. He rejects the load of lettuce and sends it back.

Go ahead and laugh...it is funny. Seems like a no brainer because if you leave the lettuce on the side track, it probably will look poorly when you inspect it after a few days. Almost sounds as if the inspector was setting the shipper up. Not really. The inspector was suspicious of the load when it arrived and just allowed it to become obvious. So it should be with our thought process when considering important matters. Let it sit...it doesn't have to be decided right this minute. That's impulse buying and salespeople love it. Instead, consider the matter, and then decide. That careful consideration will lead to having made a more informed choice.

Sure, sometimes you will decide to buy it anyway even though you really don't NEED it. Hey, that's okay. We all deserve a little pampering. At least you will have considered the consequences and you have no one to blame but yourself. This is responsibility. You know what you can afford...now make the right choice. If the choice is to treat yourself; you can and should feel good about it.

I'll talk about money, investing, and health care elsewhere, but for now I just want to address the decision-making process itself. Things that you need to know and consider:

1. **What specifically do I need to decide?** You need to know what you're deciding about. Sounds obvious but consider this. Let's say you have $5,000. You have several investments, but this specific $5,000 is up for decision. It is money that you don't need presently in a non-interest or low-interest bearing account to pay bills like your checking, but you would like to make a little money from it, but yet have it available because you anticipate some large bills coming in over the next few months. That information will lead you toward a certain decision.

2. **What are the choices?** You have accounts at the local Credit Union. There is checking (where the money is now), money market, and long-term savings. You also have the means to buy stocks funds, or bonds. What choice fits the need?

3. **What are the pros and cons of all the choices?** The checking earns no interest. The money market earns a small percentage. The long-term saving earns more, but is restricted as to the number of annual withdrawals you can make. Stocks and bonds may earn more, but you want fast access to this money because it is part of your emergency cash or what you might call "I need the money now fund" in case the washer and dryer blow up.

4. **Narrow the choices down to two or three.** So, I'm down to the bank accounts: checking, money market,

and long-term savings, if I want fast access. Checking earns nothing as I said, money market earns a small amount of interest, and the long-term savings earns more...also the more I put in long term savings the more I earn on a tiered basis and putting the $5,000 there would up my percentage a bit on all of the money in that account at least for a few months. The long-term account restricts my withdrawals to five per year, but I am unlikely to exceed that anyway. In a catastrophe, I would remove all of what I need in one shot.

5. Select **the best of the three and don't look back.** So, it looks like I put the money in my long-term savings and watch it grow a little faster instead of leaving in parked in my checking account where it is earning nothing. As a caveat to my first writing; I have since found a checking account that pays more interest than my savings up to a certain limit. I could now let this money stay in the checking, have instant access, and earn interest.

If I keep on making these types of smart money moves, I can eventually move to longer term investments once I exceed my emergency fund amount. Now, that took a while to type on my computer, but if you are familiar with your bank accounts and have chosen them wisely, this decision would not take long at all and you would be done with it and on to something else after you have made the money transfer using your on-line banking access. Not that you made a snap decision and went after the highest interest rate without thinking, but you ended up making the most money you can with the least risk and the availability that you wanted. This might not seem like much because you will make maybe $20, but its $20 you can now spend. Over several years, it will make a difference and spending someone else's money is always better than spending your own.

If you keep on the lookout for good ideas, read about financial matters and listen to others that you trust, you too can become smart about making decisions and being confident that they are good ones. Don't go for perfect. You will never make a move. Rather go for what is good for you and don't be talked into anything that is good simply because it is popular.

Never be pressured into a decision. If a salesman tells you the price on anything is only good until you walk out the door...walk. This is part of a high-pressure game and you don't want to play. Honest deals are truly negotiable and reputable salespeople will always allow you to think it over or consult with your spouse. If you feel like you are in a corner...walk, but leave your phone number if you really are interested. They will be calling you.

The way to get into a pressure situation is to put yourself into it because you are not prepared. If you are shopping for a new computer or a new car; do your homework. Know what you want and what you are willing to pay. It is always better to be shopping when you don't need something immediately. I know it's hard to do all the time, but we need to cut down on our impulse buying as a nation. That will make us smarter consumers and bring runaway spending under control. This goes for governments as well as individuals.

Chapter 18: Rehearsal

And a one and a two...

Okay. So you have made a plan, selected your retirement date, saved what you estimated you need and are well on your way to achieving your goal. You have been smart in caring for your money, protected your retirement fund, and maximized your earnings without taking unnecessary chances. It is now three to five years before your selected retirement date and you are on track to reach your goal...the question now is; will your carefully laid plan work? Have you made the right decisions, calculations, and predictions? This is a good time to try it out...while you still have time to make some changes...either to save more, change the date, or as the kids say...whatever.

The exercise here is to try out your retirement plan with the income you expect and the bills you anticipate in retirement. First, make a list of all of the income you expect in retirement. (You should really already have this, but this is a good place to update it.) Pensions, annuities, social security, if you are eligible and you're going to take it. Also include 3% or 4% of your nest egg (or dividend income depending on your plan) that you have been carefully building to supplement your other income. Divide this by 12 and this is what will flow into your checkbook every first of the month during retirement. Next, you need a list of all of your expenses. That is: utilities, insurances, taxes, healthcare, cell phone and land line, investments, magazine subscriptions, groceries, cable...everything you can think of and reduce it to a per month cost. This can take a few months to accumulate a good average...it may take up to a year to be really accurate. Then, compare the two…your income should be more than your outlay…the difference is your play money. Discretionary income should be maybe two to three thousand dollars every month in excess of expenses. Then try to live on exactly what you have computed for up to a year…save the rest. This trial also helps you to save a bundle of cash and beef up your accounts and emergency fund. Just live out of your "retirement income" amount by diverting just that amount from your paycheck into your checking account and the rest into long-term savings.

The "fun" part of this is that by living on just 60-70% of your income, your long term savings will grow at a rapid rate. By doing this for an extended time, you may find that you don't really need as much in your retirement…so just reduce the amount you are taking…or you might need a little more…this can probably be done without pain because your long-term savings is growing faster than you planned anyway. So, the rehearsal can fine tune your planning in either regard.

Give this rehearsal some time. You will probably miss a few expenses. Add them in and adjust the figures in your list. Also, if you're like us, not every month's expenses are the same. Many bills are paid on an annual or quarterly basis. Property taxes and insurance for example are often quarterly or annual payments. Sometimes a given month…it's June for us…expenses are very high. In those months, I take money for my savings account to make up for the difference, just like when I was working. You can have a savings account in retirement, too. Fund it from your catch-up money initially and then transfer some money in good months from checking to savings and in poorer months, transfer it back to make up the difference. There is no way that you can make every month's expenses identical. On-line banking makes all of these manipulations a snap.

You should arrange to direct-deposit funds from your income to have just the amount you expect in retirement go into your checkbook. Have the rest go into another interest bearing account. If you think about it, this interest bearing account should accumulate quickly...this is part of your catch up fund...call it a retirement bonus (This is the 30% or 40% of your income that you are not going to have in retirement). Remember, if you are in the last throws of paying off your mortgage; that money should come from this account. Also, if you are paying off credit cards or any other loan, it should also come from this account. Are you seeing the debt-free sign yet? Hopefully you were debt free before you started this dress rehearsal for retirement but if not, this should bring you to zero-debt.

Now, try to live on just what you think you will have in retirement and see how it feels. If it works, then in three to five years it should be no problem comfortably slipping into that retirement pay. If you are finding yourself short every month, you need to adjust your sights. Maybe save a little more, arrange for an annuity before you retire, or work a little longer. Make the adjustment and move on. It is better to know now, before you call it quits, than later when you can't do much about it and you find yourself applying for that greeter's job at Wal-Mart just to make ends meet.

That interest bearing account could be the key to getting it right. Accumulating that extra cushion might be just enough to correct the error. I remember sitting at a work meeting on a Saturday. It was in February. No one wanted to be there and the heat was not on in the building. The subject matter was fairly interesting, but we were not getting paid and it was cold. It was just one of those things where you had to go...sort of a grin and bear it...more like a shiver and bear it that day.

So there I was sitting next to friend and I decided to check my portfolio balance. I had not looked for maybe a week...don't look every day...it will make you crazy. In my retirement plan, I needed $500K in my portfolio in addition to my pensions to retire. I needed that much despite our pensions because we would only be collecting a portion of our full pensions. I would get 39% and my wife would get 41% based on our years of service. So, that is an average of 40% of our take home. I needed the other 20%. About 8% would come from my National Guard retirement. I'm up to 48% but I'm still 12% short. That's why I needed the $500K to draw on.

So, there I was...a bit bored, cold and a little down because I had to be there at all. My friend told me later that he had glanced over and saw me checking my email and some other things and then there was a moment.

I use a free on-line portfolio to keep track of my investments, profits, losses, etc. There is one box that provides a total worth of the contents of the portfolio. My friend tells me that when I saw this, a smile came to my face and a look of peace came over me. I had made it. I knew I could retire at the end of the school year. There was just the matter of discussing it with my wife and if she was also ready to retire because she had made it very clear some time ago that she would retire first or we would retire together...but I definitely would not retire first while she continued to work. That summer was our target date from years ago, but I was sure that it would come as a surprise as the actual words were spoken that we were ready.

After some discussion and hand wringing, we decided to do it. My wife would retire in June at the end of the school year and I would follow in August. To have the decision made was a great relief. There is no feeling like knowing you're close to the end when you go back to work...the only trouble was it was too early to reveal our plans and become a lame duck. So, we waited to tell even our closest friends...but we were certainly ready and our rehearsal had put the money discussions behind us.

Chapter 19: I Quit

Deciding to pack it in.

Finally, let's get to it. Leaving your job for retirement may seem like a simple thing. I include it here because I believe I did not do it well and have paid some price for my inattentiveness. I thought it was a mere slide out the side door, but it's more than that and I could have done it better. The effect of your leaving reaches out to many that surround you. It affects them in different ways and everyone needs time to deal with it. No one is irreplaceable, but in the replacement many are affected, some in more ways than you may ever realize.

First, once you make the decision to leave, it is only you that knows. Don't believe that anyone else is paying attention because it really doesn't matter to them. Well, it does because it may mean something to their job situation. I think that part of my problem was considering what my retirement would mean to my own status…i.e. lame duck…that drove my secrecy and not sharing it with others. I was worried that my announcement would create an uncomfortable situation but more than that, I didn't think it would matter to others all that much. I kept my decision under wraps for a long time until I finally had to inform certain people to finalize the process.

Well, I found out that your leaving does matter for many others. There are friends and allies that you have made through your career that wish you well. And they would like to rejoice with you and you need to give them that chance. The positive emotional supports that you will gain from those good wishes will more than make up for the ill will that others will send your way as a lame duck. Even if you are giving up authority in say six months...what does it matter that you start losing it now? It is irrelevant. But the emotional support, ah, that would have been priceless.

I once tried to slide out of position of authority earlier in my career by transferring responsibility before I left because I thought it would be a good thing for the company. I wasn't quitting the company; I just anticipated a reassignment and wanted someone to take over before my departure. I thought I could help in the transition by being there...wrong! Higher ups saw it as me quitting...side-stepping responsibility. Not trying to help, but rather trying to ease my own situation. No amount of explaining could convince them otherwise and it hurt my advancement for awhile.

The point I learned from that was to work in your assignment until management feels that you are worthy of promotion. At that point it will happen and your supervisors will not be concerned about the transfer of responsibility. So, let them worry about it. I tried to use this logic about my retirement, but it is not the same.

Once you decide to retire, it is best to let those in authority know. Start with your immediate supervisor and work your way up as is appropriate. Inform Human Resources if you are in a company that has that department and go from there. Let the chips fall where they may and try to leave without burning any bridges. You have worked with these people for a long time and by and large they all wish you well. So give them the chance to express it. It will feel good; for you and for them.

Oh, I'm not so naïve to believe that everyone wishes you well. But it doesn't matter. No one will be able to take a parting shot without looking foolish. After all, you are the one who has made it…who could argue with that?

Leaving is a big change for you, too. There may be twenty or thirty years of work and emotion invested and there are some strong feelings involved in leaving all of that behind. Consider those feelings. If you have close allies at work, talk it over with them. They can help you with coping with the loss. Yes, it is a loss. You have earned plenty of things by your work, not just money, and you are walking away from it. There will be a feeling of loss and you do need to privately mourn it.

It is hard to imagine that last day as you walk away and you don't have to come back tomorrow. For me, it was during the summer months and as a school principal there was no one else around. I took one last walk around the building, ensuring it was secure. I laid the master key to the building in the center of my ink blotter, set the security code into the alarm system, and exited the door. The door closed behind me and I did not have the key to re-enter. It was over.

You have put in a great deal of effort to attain what you have in your job. The education and the long hours of work have brought you to this point. You are at the top of your career and here you are walking away. It seems counterintuitive, but don't lose sight of what the goal truly is. The goal is independence; remember… a thing called retirement where your money pays you, not the other way around. You have reached that point. There should be a feeling of great joy, release, and freedom like emerging from your cocoon, sprouting your wings, and flying freely into your next phase.

Chapter 20: Investing after Retirement
Am I out of the game?

I have devoted considerable space in these writings to saving and accumulating enough money to finance your retirement. But what happens to your investment plan once you do retire? You have all of this money invested and saved, what do you do with it now to protect what you have worked so hard for and maybe even make a little bit more?

I have not discussed my own Social Security benefit to this point. Now might be a good time to discuss it. My wife and I were both 63 as of the original writing of this manuscript and neither of us had taken our Social Security Retirement benefit. My Social Security will never amount to thousands, but only a few hundred dollars per month because the federal government in its infinite wisdom has decided that those who have a defined benefit pension from a state or federal source as we do will be penalized a sizable chunk of their Social Security benefit (WEP). How about that? I qualify and have paid in what others have, but I don't get it because I paid more money into another pension plan. Anyway, I would only earn about $500 per month after that penalty. You might want to check yours which is probably considerably more...go to www.socialsecurity.gov and you can calculate your own benefit. You don't need to know anything, just your social security number. Yes, they know everything about you.

My wife does not qualify for her own social security benefit because she lacks the qualified quarters; neither does she qualify for half of mine because of the same penalty. Why didn't I grab the social security benefit at 63? I'm in relatively good health and social security earnings increase by 8% for every year I don't take it. Also, at that point I didn't need it so it was like an investment earning 8% per year. Hard to beat in this market so I left it alone. I couldn't beat that growth percentage presently in any bank.

When I turned 65, I seriously thought about cashing in my Social Security benefit. What prompted this thinking; Medicare. Before your 65th birthday, everyone must sign up for Medicare. If you are still working and receive benefits from your employer, you need only sign up for Part A, which is free. If you are no longer working, you must sign up for Part B, which costs presently $134 per month or $1604 per year. These bills now come every three months for me and my wife...a nuisance... especially if we are traveling. I found out that I can sign up for automatic payment, but it is not possible to accomplish this on line. You can download the form, fill it out, mail it in, and maybe in 6-8 weeks they may start the automatic deductions. Jeez...really, in this day and age?

So, I finally took my Social Security benefit at my full retirement age (66) because the Medicare payments would be automatically deducted from that benefit every month. I will give up the next four years of benefit growth, but the benefit is not getting huge growth because it isn't that big to begin with. I have read recently that there is a bill on the floor of the House to eliminate the penalty for those with a retirement plan like mine. Hooray. The bill in its present form will also be retroactive. I'm not holding my breath.

I also have some cash that I have been using for the last four or five years to back up my pension and act as an emergency fund. I have not really dipped into this either so what I do is ladder the investments. Banks and credit unions will usually give you more interest the longer the term you invest. That is a one year investment might bring a 1% return where a five-year investment might bring more than double that. This is more of what I call my immediate available cash. So, what I do is spread out these investments. That is I invest some for 1 year, some for two years, etc. up to five years. As the first year matures, I either take some (I have not) or reinvest it for five years usually at a higher interest rate. So, every year I have an investment maturing and a decision to make. It's comforting to know I always have a big chunk of money maturing that I can use...can you say an update to the car or motor home?

This has worked out quite well. Last year was the first time that I took the interest from the CD as profit, put it in my checking account as income, and reinvested the principal in another 5-year CD to continue the ladder. In the coming years, the profits increase because of the longer investment, and I will do the same thing. So, my ready-cash-reserve remains the same amount and I can spend the profits. This was not my idea. Remember I said that other people have good ideas, too? Well, this was one of them I read about in *Bottom Line Personal*.

The ladder CD's was the basic plan at the beginning of my retirement and has worked out well, but lately things have changed. CD rates are fluctuating and right now are a bit upside down. By that I mean that some short term CD's are paying a higher rate than longer term CD's. I know that's a bit crazy, but that's the way it is. So, for the last two years, I have rolled over my investments into two-year CD's because they are paying a higher rate right now than 5-year CD's. When it comes time for rollover, I'll have to pay attention each time to the prevailing rates.

I knew I was going to be a bit short of what I wanted to collect monthly in my retirement over twenty years ago according to my ballpark figure. One of the ways I was planning to make this up was through an annuity. I also thought I would have to pay for my own health care, but my Uncle Sam took care of that with my TriCare benefit. So, let's talk about that cash I was saving to bankroll my health care and annuity.

An annuity looked good several years ago when the interest rates were much higher, now they don't look so good and you have to give up the principle. As an explanation, an annuity is an income plan where you give an insurance company a chunk of cash and they give it back to you monthly with interest. Many of these plans are for life so you are betting that you will collect more than you gave and the insurance company is betting you won't. Meanwhile, they have your cash to invest. I was planning on a $100,000 annuity that would pay me about $800 per month. Now you're lucky if you can get $650 per month out of $100,000 annuity. Since I didn't have to use the cash for healthcare and I didn't purchase the annuity, I invested some of the cash and widened the scope of my portfolio and banked the rest for my emergency fund. I'm now resting comfortably, thanks. The bulk of that cash was still earning 4% in the 403b which I can keep, but I had to start drawing down according to federal law when I'm 70. *I wrote the previous paragraph in the first edition and carried it through to the second. Now...you read what happened to this money in The Big Mistake chapter. I don't regret it and we enjoy the lake house very much. With the improvements we have made, I'm sure I could recoup that loss, but more than likely it will never happen because the lake house will never be sold in my lifetime, but rather passed down to my children.*

So my situation is this. I planned to pay for my own health care and I didn't need to so I saved that money. I of course over-planned for my monthly income so I have extra money there. Also it turns out that I don't spend as much in retirement as I thought even with all the traveling we do. So, all that adds up to...I have extra cash *even after the big mistake.*

What about my stock portfolio now that I'm retired? Because I have a guaranteed income stream and I now have extra cash, I can afford to take a little risk here. Not a lot mind you, but a little. I am a buy and hold type of investor as I have told you and I still am. I don't involve myself in day trading. I learned my lesson with that a long time ago. I maintain my portfolio of dividend reinvestment accounts as I did before I retired. I have even added to it and rebalanced it. I no longer contribute to my investments every month because I wanted to increase my monthly income.

So, I have cash in the form of dividends held by my broker, investment CD's, and a stock portfolio backing up my defined benefit pension and paying me every month. I have a safety net with social security and adjustments I can make to my savings habits that will give me more spendable cash. I have upgraded my ride to a 2014 Mustang from my 2005, my wife still drives a 2008 Honda, and we have upgraded to a 2012 Fleetwood Bounder motor home. Many of you may be saying why, why, why? Get a new car...get a new motor home...live it up...you can afford it. And you would be right. I can afford it.

But we want to travel and sleep at night and also leave a legacy to our kids. (I'll write more on leaving a legacy later.) Yes, we can afford it. But we have enough and everything is maintained in tip-top condition. The cars do not break down and are in good shape. We keep them well-maintained and they continue to serve us well.

There it is again, *enough*. The newer motor home is well maintained and runs like a top...and we have not found anything we like better...yes, we have looked and five years later we did find something we liked better. We used to have a 2003 motor home, but it was getting worn so you see we have upgraded to a 2012. I can't say that they make them better though. We upgraded because we had put a lot of miles on the 2003 in our retirement and it was starting to show some serious wear. The new Bounder sure is more comfortable, but it drives me crazy with all the little things that go wrong with it all of the time. The motor home manufacturers are making them lighter, but I think that means, less tough. The older one was an "iron" but it sure could stand up to the punishment. Over the last couple of years I have been over the Bounder from stem to stern and we have made friends...as long as it continues to behave.

The Mustang is my toy which I drive all of 2,500 miles per year with the top down and the wind blowing through my more than ever thinning hair. It is just a little expense (Insurance & Taxes) for so much fun. We also take trips to the beach and some fall trips in New England using the Mustang. My wife always carries a blanket and a jacket in the convertible because she knows I seldom put the top up. The Honda we tow behind the motor home and it accumulates only about 5,000 miles per year actual driving miles, runs great, and I wouldn't want to buy something new just to subject it to all that punishment of being towed behind the motor home. So it's all enough. It does what we want, performs well, looks good, and fulfills our needs…oh, so you see I'm not out to impress anyone else…"You can't please everyone so you've got to please yourself." (Thanks for that advice, Ricky.)

Retirement does not remove you from the investing game. Some of your money is, but you are not. If I look at my total worth, including my defined benefit plan, I'm less than 35% invested in stocks. Oh, I haven't sold anything, but I have significantly added to my cash holdings. My aforementioned defined benefit plan is now mine to spend every month and changes the balance of my entire portfolio. I will not need the principal of my portfolio to live on right now and the way I look at it maybe never. (See *Living on Someone Else's Money.*) I'm living the good life on less than I "ball parked" so I'm "flush" as they say and that portfolio is now well within my risk allowance. In fact 35% in stocks is rather on the conservative side. I have had some fabulous growth in my stock portfolio over the last eight years and that growth paid for my updated Mustang and RV and added value to my holdings, so I may be up to 45% in stocks, but really…at this point, I'm playing with the "House's" money.

And you are burning to ask the question, why didn't this guy have a broker? Simple…I hate fees. Oh, I paid some fees as I invest each month, but they were a one-time occurrence and actually quite a pittance. I couldn't see paying some guy 1% of the money I have already made every year. It galls me to think that these guys are collecting money on the money that others have earned. This is part of the selling of fear that I was speaking of earlier. Could they save me a few bucks by being shrewd with the rules...sure...but then I turn around and give them twice as much. I used to get many calls from brokers telling me about how well they could do for me in the market. My first question was how old they were...the second was...if they are so smart about money...how come they aren't retired? I don't want to be in your movie and I already read the book...Have a nice day.

You have read earlier that I now have a broker/financial advisor. I think I have to be smarter about how a withdraw money from my accounts as I might need it and certainly those rules are complicated. Also, the single broker's statement makes it much easier to fill out my taxes. Because I am not trading stocks, my fees are extremely low for all the services that I get.

Taking care of your money and continuing to grow your legacy in retirement is as important as accumulating enough wealth to get there in the first place. Sure, you cannot take the chances you once did as you were investing and you must reduce your risk factors, but there are plenty of "safe" investments to keep your money working for you because the next goal is not only taking care of yourself and your spouse, but creating that legacy for your kids and your grandkids. No, I don't want my last check to bounce and say I spent all that I earned. Instead I want my children and my grandchildren to enjoy what I have and provide the springboard for them to get there and beyond.

Yes, my original goal was to take care of my wife and me in our retirement. Accumulate a great income stream and enjoy all of it until there wasn't any more. Hopefully, that event would occur just as we didn't need it anymore. But a funny thing happened. Because I over planned and don't need as much as I thought in retirement, my goals have changed. I started thinking of a future beyond us and even beyond our kids. I thought about what truly wealthy families do and thought, "Why not us?" Why can't our family have a chunk of cash that is passed down and provides a legacy of stress-free living to future generations? Hey, a guy can dream.

Chapter 21: Leaving it to Your Kids

The making of your grandchildren...

We all desire to raise our children to be successful in their work and in personal lives. Like most parents, we attempted to give our children every advantage. Of course through their teenage years they thought we were the dumbest people on the planet. I'm sure they are amazed at how much we have learned since that time. It's an old story...youth is wasted on the young, but it always has been and there is no use in complaining about it.

So, now our kids are grown with those wonderful little creatures...grandchildren have arrived; ah, the wonders of grandchildren. No worries about spoiling them now; it's your job. No real concerns about counseling them; your example is their counsel. The stars are aligned. But I don't feel that my job is done as far as my children or my grandchildren are concerned. There are plenty of years remaining and well and I won't be around for all of it; I fear. But we sure would like to continue providing that *advantage* for them we have been talking about.

A legacy is something we can leave; a legacy in the form of peace; a legacy in the form of money and wisdom. Not so much money that they can live off of it and squander it, but a legacy to enable them to do what we have done for ourselves. They can also hopefully do for their children what I will do for them; the fact that they will have enough money to be comfortable and pursue their dreams is very satisfying to me. So, in their life they will not have to worry, but there will always be a cushion to spring them up in tough times, but I see this as coming with a heavy responsibility for them.

The responsibility is that the legacy is not only for their peace of mind, but for the peace of mind of their children, our grandchildren, our great grandchildren, and beyond. Our children will now be responsible to give their children every opportunity and more and that they may do the same for their grandchildren. That's right...the legacy of responsibility...they will become the caretakers of the wealth of the family. They must pass on what they have been given and more. I don't want a statue, but I have been given many gifts from my immigrant grandparents and my first generation American-born parents and I feel that those gifts must not stop with me.

So much for the soap box speech, let's get down to how we do this. First, you don't want to give all that you have to the state or to the federal government in the form of death or inheritance taxes. What I plan to do very shortly, and I will need some legal assistance to do this right, is to form a trust. A trust owned by my wife and I and then by my children. All that my wife and I own upon our passing will be deposited in that trust and given to our children. There will be very little that will be subject to any tax, if I execute this properly.

I cannot take credit for this idea. It is my in-laws that were counseled to do this and it worked like a charm. My sister-in-law was the executor, a job that she performed admirably. The house was sold, accounts were cashed in, banks were notified, and everything except two annuities were deposited into the trust and distributed. It was legal tax genius and I plan to set up the same for my children with a bit of a different strategy.

The more difficult part of the plan is the legacy. That is that the accumulation of wealth stay as a large investment, actually in two chunks...one for each of our children, providing security for whoever is its trustee at the moment (like myself or Pat) and then passing it along to the next generation to provide the cushion of comfort for each succeeding generation with the same purchasing power with which they received it.

The point is that they should grow the trust to pass on to their children. It is acceptable that they spend the market gain from the trust as we have, but the point is to grow the principal before it is passed on to the succeeding generation. This will have to be done by influence more than decree. Each succeeding generation will have to become money smart and work hard to replenish and grow the legacy and divide it for the next group. In theory it should be easier for them because they are starting with a sizable account that is already earning its own income. All they have to do is add to it. Such are the things of dreams.

The problem is that the original legacy always gets diluted. That is; it is divided by the number of children you have. Let's say that each family needs X amount of cash to retire along with pensions and social security. OK. In your lifetime, for the sake of this discussion, let's say you live off your pension and social security and never touch X. So, in my case I pass down to my children, two of them, X/2. This means they are already half-way to their retirement/financial comfort savings. So, at the least they only have to accumulate half as much as I have to pass down X to their two children...who again get X/2, and so it goes.

Hopefully, each succeeding generation accumulates more than X/2 and they pass down X+. This would enhance the legacy and each succeeding generation would get more. In this way, the family would always be wealthy. Not wealthy in the sense that they never have to work, but wealthy enough to be not anxious about money, but they will have to make their own way. They will have enough assets to do what they want in their work and the means to achieve it. Now aren't you glad you paid attention in that algebra class?

I speak of wealth and for most people that means money. I really don't see it as money, but as peace of mind. I can live off my pensions and social security quite well, thank you, but the peace of mind brought on by the extra in my savings and portfolio is priceless. It is the peace of mind in knowing that I always have a backup. There is always something there for an emergency and that a money crisis is not any part of my worry. That is the legacy I want for my children and grandchildren.

My aging Mother at this moment has come to rely on her children to help support her in decisions and assistance with money matters. When it comes to money, there is nothing that can divide a family faster. When my Mom's bills come due both my sister and I assist her with getting them paid. Oh, she still keeps her budget envelopes up-to-date and is self sufficient with money, but occasionally needs help with getting the bills done and dealing with insurance companies and the like. I do not have to worry about my checking account balance even with this extra pressure. It is that cushion I speak of that provides this comfort and when dealing with matters such as these, it is priceless.

What price would you be willing to pay for this kind of peace? It isn't a high price at all. It's a bit of frugality and not having all of the latest and the greatest, immediately. It is in the rejoicing in what you have, not what you desire. I'm never saying that you should not work toward something you want, but rather you should do just that. "Work" toward something you want and then relish the joy in achieving it.

So, almost ten years later I am feeling good about my retirement plan and its results. The portfolio has grown beyond what I thought it would and I really am living off my pensions and the dividends of our accumulated portfolio. I have little desire to go out and spend and accumulate any more material things. I am feeling that I need to do some work on my house to secure that living space for our advancing age. I can do less heavy work myself and thus must rely on others which will cost.

Also, we have changed what we think about leaving the children something only in the end. Oh, I'm not giving them everything now...they are too young and will squander it through their lack of wisdom. They have to struggle a bit first to acquire the sage knowledge of what to do once they get it. But, we see that we can help out along the way to ease the burden of getting there...occasionally.

We have taken to giving larger birthday and Christmas gifts. Not larger in the way of OMG, but larger in the way of something large enough to be able to buy something they need without struggling to get it. We pay attention to their needs during the year and try to anticipate some major expenses that they may be incurring. Then, just at the right time, we give them enough to help out and make it easier. It is nice to see and hear what they have done for themselves and their families with the money.

This lesson came from my wife's grandmother. At one point she decided to leave her legacy to her grandchildren in the form of a Christmas gift. Her only stipulation was that the grandchildren had to tell her what they did with the money that she had given them. We used it as part of the down payment on our house. It wasn't that we would have not bought the house if she had not given us the money, but by having a larger down payment, our mortgage payments were less for twenty years. We remembered her fondly every time we wrote the mortgage check.

Chapter 22: Can You Do This?

Dare to dream?

If you read the newspapers, magazines, and follow the online blogs; predictions continue to be dire concerning retirement for future beneficiaries. The doomsday types have old folks standing in breadlines, donning blue smocks, and practicing their "Welcome to Wal-Mart" smiles. It doesn't have to be that way and hey, what's wrong with working at Wal-Mart anyway?

The image they are representing is not the way this generation is retiring. For the most part they are motivated and active. They travel and yes work; some starting their new business after they retire. Welcome to the new *active* retirement.

The total replacement of your working income during retirement is not necessary. The retirement sages have you replacing 80% or more of your working salary in order to maintain your lifestyle. As far as I can see, this 80% figure is too high. There are things you did while working that you do not need to do during retirement such as raising children and buying a house. You are talking about two people living debt-free and enjoying themselves. That doesn't take the income you once made while working. Take away those responsibilities and the burden of saving for retirement and you can actually live on a little over half of what you were actually making.

If your lifestyle was extravagant in the first place, you were probably living over your head and need to accomplish many of the lessons in the preceding chapters before you can retire debt-free. Your last five working years will be a major course correction, not just an adjustment. Good luck with that. It can be done, but it will take a major effort and attitude adjustment on your part, but it will be worth it in the end. If you got that late a start, it is going to be tough.

Another advantage of the doomsday scenario according to the financiers is that you will save more money if you let them invest your money. Remember, they get a portion of that money every year regardless of whether you make a profit or not...the more you save, the more they make. Sure, you need some backup over exactly what you need to cover expenses, but let's be reasonable here. Unless you are looking to buy a yacht and keep an extra Lexus on the dock for side trips, about 60-70% of your former income is more than enough to maintain your lifestyle. In fact if you are debt free in retirement, 70% would provide a luxurious lifestyle. The more reasonable target is 60% of your former take home pay and being debt free.

It is sad that many people do not save an adequate amount for their retirement. They have lived hand-to-mouth and pay check to pay check for a long time and are relying on someone, maybe the government, to save them in the end. Sorry to break the news, but it's not going to happen. *"God bless the child that's got his own."* If you are waiting for some sugar daddy to come along and either show you how or provide in the end, repeat after me, "Welcome to Wal-Mart."

I have made working at WalMart in your retirement the brunt of a few of my jokes, but not everyone that works at Wal-Mart is doing so because they have to...many want to. There is a lot of time between waking and sleeping and some people need to fill their day. Some need to see other people in the course of their life because they do not have a spouse to share it with or hobbies to work at. There are many reasons for wanting to interact with others...some are just not as lucky as we have been.

Just a word about that before I go on. There are many things you can do to make your own luck, but it only goes so far. You can plan your finances and the company has a downsizing event just after you turn fifty years old...not good. You can have the greatest relationship with a spouse and an illness takes that away and you find yourself alone. Tragedy can befall anyone no matter what plans you have made. The intervention of events can be called luck if it's good or fate can intervene and it's not so good. So, just when you think you see the light at the end of the tunnel, listen, it might be a train bearing down on you. If you make it with your health, your family, and your finances...you've made it...as luck would have it.

As I'm finishing this up, I'm sitting at the beach at the end of a seven-week motor home trip thinking about what we have done and the places we have visited. Because I'm writing this, I'm also thinking about finances. The trip is all paid for. Many of my bills are automated because we are away so much. Once you leave home for more than a month, you need to have some things worked out or you fall behind. Oh, I certainly keep track. I receive emails about all the bills that are paid automatically from my checking account. With electronic banking this has been made quite easy and with no fees.

Back to my claim that the trip is all paid for; the motor home I'm riding in is paid for. The gas I've used is charged to my rewards credit card and according to the email, that bill has been paid. We use our debit card for other incidentals and that is paid directly and immediately from my checking account. We also took some cash along to pay for incidentals. So, all in all, checking my accounts, we have more money in there than I started the trip with.

"How is that," you say. Well, around the first of the month, the checks from our retirement accounts were direct-deposited into the checking account. Of course I was keeping track and as of the first of the month, we had about 10% more in the account than we started last month with. Yes, we went out to eat and did many things during our trip, but it doesn't cost all that much to have a good time. I've even learned to put my own salt on the rim of our margarita glasses. It is now considered a life skill that I cannot live without.

Yes, you can do this, too. Save over the long term, save a lot during the "catch up" period after your children are grown. Take advantage of tax breaks. Rehearse your retirement. Once you know you can do it...ride off into the sunset and don't look back.

Chapter 23: Programs, Supports, and Interventions

Help is there, if you want it.

As you probably have surmised, I am not a bleeding heart liberal. I believe in standing on your own two feet, advocating for yourself, and not relying on others to do things you can do. Having said that, there are many in our government that are very liberal in their thinking and to help everyone out, help themselves, and garner as many votes as they can for their own reelection have passed laws that are advantageous to the ordinary citizen. I'm not above taking advantage of those programs. I may be independent, but I'm not stupid.

First, there are numerous organizations like AARP that offer seniors 10% discounts on many purchases. For that matter there are many establishments that offer 10% discounts to any senior. Now, something like a 10% discount may not seem like much, and it isn't. If you make a $20 purchase that's $2 off. The two dollars won't break you, but if you do it 10 times in a year that's $20 and you just paid for a magazine subscription for the whole year. But senior discounts are offered everywhere and you would well to take advantage of them 100 or 200 times per year...well, you get the idea.

Then there are senior menus. I don't know about you, but I can't eat like I used to...I want to, but I just can't. If I get a full-size meal, I often have to lug it home where it languishes in the fridge until it looks like a junior high science experiment and then I throw it away. Instead I order from the senior or lighter fare menu. These portions are smaller and they cost less. You can still leave a big tip if you want too, but I leave feeling satisfied and with a few more bucks still left in my pocket. If you must, enjoy a cordial from the top shelf. You've earned it.

Get yourself a good cash-back credit card. You can get a reward card if you use the sky miles, but I don't fly much anymore so I go strictly for the cash. If you get a top notch card like American Express Blue Cash, they also watch your charges as you travel and offer excellent fraud protection. I've had my card number stolen and fraudulent charges made. American Express catches it before I do and sends an email. The charges are immediately removed. The card pays cash-back at different levels and at some time during the year I usually just apply the rewards to my bill. Hey, last year that was over $400. You can also purchase things with your rewards. All of this costs me nothing because I pay my bill in full every month.

My military discount is also a big saver. Some discounts apply to all that have served, but I'm talking about retired military discounts. Last year my local race car track offered a free night to all retired military veterans, a $40 value. Many eateries such as Texas Roadhouse offer free and half-priced meals. Military retirees can also use military base facilities just as they did when they were active duty. One of the benefits I use is camping on military bases at their FamCamps. The rates are reduced and the facilities are great. We also feel very secure camping on the bases protected by 10,000 Marines and we meet many other military veterans.

As much as I like using the military base facilities that greatly reduce my travel costs, I also love getting that check in the mail every month from my National Guard retirement. This helps to supplement our income and will pass to my wife just like any other retirement should something happen to me. But the absolute biggest benefit we have received from my military service is health care. As I told you before, I may have given up one weekend per month as a young man for twenty years, but it was also one of the greatest experiences of my life and now pays one of the biggest dividends. For an additional $110 per month, paired with our Medicare, my wife and I received full-benefit health care including dental and prescription drug coverage for life. Between ages 60 and 65 this was $60 per month for full coverage without Medicare. It is the one thing that made my early retirement decision easy. As my wife and I turned sixty-five we signed up for Medicare and our military insurance became our secondary carrier for prescription drugs and co-pays. So now, like all seniors, we pay for Medicare Part B...but Tricare for Life is our extended plan...a great savings.

My city also offers tax benefits to seniors. For those over 65, there is a real estate tax break for those that live in their own home. There is also a real estate tax break for veterans. Check with your city or town to see if they offer this tax relief for seniors. If you no longer own your own home, check if the tax break can be applied to your vehicle taxes or rent.

Resale shops have become a big thing lately. If you go to one in a great neighborhood, designer labels fill the shelves...some with the original tags still on them. There is a certain itch to buy things on a regular basis and with all this time on your hands, you can overdo it. But shopping at these types of stores not only benefits the organizations they serve, but scratches that itch on a regular basis.

I could go on and on about how to be frugal in your life and in your retirement, but it all comes down to keeping your eyes open. Offers abound seeking out your business. As you read the paper, scan your computer, or flip through magazines, look for the offers that are seeking you out. You don't really care if you have to go on a Tuesday or a Wednesday, typical slow nights at a restaurant, you don't have to work the next day anyway! Any night can be date night.

You have money now, but why give it away. You have the time to seek out the best buy and comparison shop...computers make it easy. There is no settling because you are tired of looking. If you don't buy today, businesses will come chasing you tomorrow with an even better deal. If you search on your computer for an item, they're probably tracking you anyway and you will receive better offers in your email the next day.

Also, do not stop tracking your retirement savings and investments. Every month I evaluate what we have spent and what we have to spend the next month. This is as easy as balancing your checkbook right after the pensions checks are deposited. That way you can see the amount of money you ended the month with and what you are starting with in the new month. You can easily pick up on a trend if you are spending too much or have extra cash. I also track all of my accounts monthly and know the exact amount of cash I have available and the worth of my investments.

Once per year I still do a big money inventory and goal setting activity. Pretty much, I calculate my net worth. I check all accounts and make financial plans for the year. This is when I decide about transferring money or rebalancing my portfolio.

I calculate my accounts' gain/losses and know exactly where I stand financially. This usually takes about an hour and I track the gain/loss over time. I used this triple play of tracking ever since I started saving for retirement. This is my way of looking at the "big picture" of my retirement savings. Once I make these decisions, I don't have to dwell on it anymore for awhile.

It is fun to spend from your retirement accounts and know you are contributing to the economy. But remember, money you spend in your town stays in your town and benefits your town. I like shopping at the local hardware store, if I can. There are local butcher shops and vegetable stands that employ my neighbors and their families that I like to support. And don't forget the local farmers. When you're looking around at those yard sales for those once-in-a-lifetime bargains, don't forget to buy lemonade and a cookie from the little entrepreneur with the home-made stand.

Chapter 24: Is This You?

So now what?

So, what is in the cards for you? Are you willing to trust the government to provide what you need for the future or, are you ready to take your future into your own hands and determine your own fate? Are you content to lay back and let big government dictate how you will live in your retirement or are you the master of your own destiny?

You know what I chose. No one has anything coming. No one deserves it because everyone else has it. If the wealth is shared…no one is wealthy. Opportunity is what can be shared and that is what everyone has here in the USA. Everything is there; you just need to be willing to pursue it. Are you?

I know you have goals and dreams for the future in your mind. Attainment of those goals is possible. It all comes down to effort; the willingness to pursue your goals and to seek out where the opportunities lie. Don't capitulate. Your goal is out there waiting for you. You just have to find it. It does not come all at once. You need to make a plan and work toward your goal in an incremental fashion. As Rigo told us, "It don't come easy."

My wife gave my grandchildren a "dream box" that we picked up for them on one of our adventures. The directions state, "Write your dreams on a piece of paper and place it in the box and put it at your bedside. Every morning and every night, pick up your dream box and think of your dream." This all sounds like silly folklore, but I don't think it is silly at all. If you focus on your dream every morning and every night you will make plans to achieve it and seek out the means to make your dreams come true. If you have this type of determination, I have no doubt that you will succeed. I believe you will find what you are looking for and achieve any dream. If you want to learn to play the cello, it is best that at some time, you sign up for lessons.

Don't wait. The longer you put off starting saving for your retirement, the more difficult it will be. When you are young it is the easiest, so get started now. You can't think that someday you will start...someday you'll get there. If you never start, you never will get there. Time passes quickly and someday you find yourself standing there with little to show for your efforts. When you are forty, you can almost see yourself retiring and more reality sets in. This is the time most people start in earnest to save. You can do it from there, but the gift of compound interest is less on your side but hey, its 20 or 25 years until retirement...it's more than possible. Don't despair that you didn't start earlier, start today and you will get there. Lament until tomorrow and you might not.

So, in that dream box put your retirement dream. Calculate your "Ballpark Figure." What it is you want to save and what it is you want to do with your second-phase after your work life is complete? Think of that dream every morning and every night and make plans to achieve it. As luck would have it...your dream of a comfortable and productive retirement will come true.

About the Author

DJ Charpentier is a retired teacher and principal. Mr. Charpentier also served over twenty years in the Rhode Island Air National Guard. *As Luck Would Have It (First Edition)* was his first full length manuscript in which he shared his experiences concerning saving for and coping with retirement. In *5 Years Later* he updated the original writing and now in *Retire Well!* He looks back with the wisdom garnered in ten years of retirement.

Mr. Charpentier has also published six novels; three in the Reggie Slater Mystery Series and Three in the Russ Deever Mystery Series. These are also available on *Amazon.com*.

Mr. Charpentier lives is Rhode Island and travels extensively with his wife in their motor home throughout the United States. They also now enjoy the peace and tranquility of the lake house.

From the author:

I enjoy getting mail from readers and attempt to answer all email. Please, do not send snail mail. With all the traveling we do, there is no way I can answer those promptly. If you do want an answer, please send email to DPCharp@gmail.com.

Creating stories and communicating with readers is something I find extremely enjoyable and wish I had started writing years ago. I enjoy reading because a well crafted story transports you to a place and immerses you into another world. Writing does the same except you can craft that world and manipulate the characters to fit what you wish to happen. It is a lot of work, but the rewards greatly outweigh the pain.

DJ Charpentier

Acknowledgement

I want to make mention and special thank you again to my wife Pat and daughters Jess and Lori. I would also like to single out the contributions of my good friend Ernie L. that has contributed beyond his knowledge through conversations and critique to the development of this writing. They have helped my effort to produce this book in several ways, some I may not fully understand or ever realize; my thanks to you all for having the patience to put up with me.

Also, I offer my thanks to *Money Magazine* and *USA Today* and countless publications that I have read over time. The accumulated knowledge I have gained from those writings has contributed to the success of our retirement and the publication of this manuscript.